To Deni...

Teachers touch the lives of their students and affect them profoundly.

Jim Gomes

READY
SET
TEACH!

Praise for Jim Gomes'

READY-SET-TEACH!

"A delightful, refreshing, practical, and meaningful book that is guaranteed to make you laugh, sigh, and wish you would have come up with such simple yet productive tips yourself. A great read for new teachers and those who 'have been around the block a few times.' "

> —Barbara Coloroso, educator and author of five
> international bestsellers including *kids are worth it!*

"Where was Jim's book in 2003 when I was a new teacher? *Ready-Set-Teach!* is a straightforward, practical guide for any teacher at any level looking for support, motivation, and inspiration. Now that I've discovered it, this book is at the top of my resource list."

> —Jane Etherington, 10 years in education; founder
> and director, Limestone Players Travelling
> Theatre Troupe

"Any teacher who chooses to own this book will have a tremendous gift. With its emphasis on positive attitude, strong self-motivation, and complete details of how-to, one is on the way to being a great teacher."

> —R. Dale Burley, 35 years in education; department
> head, English

"You can spend a couple of decades accumulating successful teaching tips, or you can read this book and have golden nuggets of classroom management suggestions immediately available. I suggest the latter!"

—Vaughn Wadelius, 37 years in education as a teacher, elementary and high school principal, president of the Manitoba Teachers Society; currently a school board chair

"*Ready-Set-Teach!* is an invaluable resource for those entering the profession or already in it. It should be recommended, if not required, reading for people entering a Faculty of Education. It's a jewel."

—Jolene Murphy, 26 years in education, teaching for the past 10 years at Providence Care Mental Health Services-Westwood School

"This book is a go-to reference guide that is straight to the point and simple to navigate—one that efficiently states concerns, offers sound advice and effective solutions."

—Deanna Evans, teacher, 5 years in education

"All educators, regardless of whether they are classroom teachers, counsellors, special educators, or administrators, will benefit from reading *Ready-Set-Teach!* Ultimately, the real winners will be students and parents."

—Ray Ball, 37 years in education as a teacher, an administrator, and coordinator of exceptional education and guidance

READY
SET
TEACH!

101
Tips
for
Classroom
Success

JIM GOMES

Suite 300 – 990 Fort Street
Victoria, BC, Canada V8V 3K2
www.friesenpress.com

Certain names have been changed.

Copyright © 2014 by Jim Gomes
First Edition — 2014

Edited by Larry Carrick

For quantity discounts, contact
Jim Gomes at jim@JGoLearn.com

ISBN
978-1-4602-5141-6 (Hardcover)
978-1-4602-5142-3 (Paperback)
978-1-4602-5143-0 (eBook)

1. *Education, General*
2. *Education, Classroom Management*
3. *Education, Professional Development*

Distributed to the trade by The Ingram Book Company

To my mom and dad, Maria and Elson Gomes, thanks for all the sacrifices you have made on my behalf.

You will always be my heroes.

CONTENTS

ACKNOWLEDGEMENTS

Many thanks to three inspirational teachers—Mrs. Kathleen (Kaye) Arnott, Mr. Todd Romiens, and Mr. Bob Turner—whose conviction and caring set me on the path to becoming an educator.

My life's journey as a teacher would not have been the same without the unwavering support of my devoted wife Pam. Heartfelt thanks to my daughter Charlotte Gomes for her insights as an English teacher, for providing encouragement and having confidence in me from day one; to my son David Gomes for technological advice and helping me to think outside the box; and to my son Stephen Gomes for assistance in dealing with my many software and hardware issues along the way.

Special thanks to my three talented sisters: Annie Atkinson, a successful journalist, for her encouragement and professional expertise; Mary Jane Gomes, an accomplished filmmaker and photographer, for her guidance, zeal, and continued support; and Maurina Gomes for providing perspective as an elementary school music and drama teacher. I am also grateful to my niece Laurie Humphrey, a journalist, for her valuable advice, and to my brother-in-law Jim Atkinson for lending his photographic talents to this project.

It is my pleasure to thank Elizabeth Strutt-MacLeod for helping me keep my eye on what is most important and for her many worthwhile suggestions. To Dave Lynn, thank you for providing your professional observations from an administrator's point of view. Thank you also to Jim Sparrow for facilitating professional reviews, and to Rick Summers for your contract review and legal opinion on a variety of issues. It is with a deep sense of gratitude that I acknowledge my editor, Larry Carrick. His professionalism and creativity always kept me on my toes, his good judgment kept me on topic, and his humour kept me grounded.

To the thousands of students I have had the pleasure to teach: You have enriched my life immeasurably and without you this book would not have been possible.

PREFACE

Today's teachers face greater challenges than ever before and I salute all who have chosen this worthiest of professions. Teaching is a fantastic career, always demanding and rewarding at the same time—perhaps my greatest reward is that all three of my children have become teachers. A year into retirement, I still found myself drawn to the classroom, and so began the writing of this book.

During my 35 years as a full-time high school teacher, I witnessed the many struggles teachers had with classroom management. This proved to be the downfall of most who left the profession. Helping new teachers and student teachers find solutions to their problems has always been one of my greatest joys. To this end, I wish to offer teachers a leg up on many of the challenges they may encounter on a daily basis. It is my hope that student teachers, those in the early years of their careers, and even veterans will find a number of ideas and suggestions in this short book that will help them to create a happy, healthy learning environment through effective classroom management.

Although the 101 tips outlined in this book grew out of my experience teaching high school students, teachers of elementary or even post-secondary teachers will find many to be useful and rooted in best practices.

Carefully designed rules and procedures are necessary for effective classroom management, and the sooner they are in place the better. Such regimens and boundaries provide students with models of planning, thoughtfulness, and caring, reducing the number, duration, and frequency of disruptions in the classroom. This maximizes productivity and helps keep students on task, freeing up time for everyone to enjoy a creative lesson.

Though some of these tips are for use outside the classroom, each one can have a positive effect on the atmosphere inside your room. Many of these tips I created myself. Some are of the nuts and bolts variety and others I would describe as golden nuggets. Regardless, I hope you'll find them all to be useful, and I wish you both success and fulfillment throughout your teaching career.

HOW TO USE THIS BOOK

The first three chapters of this book, Preparation Strategies, Day One, and Day Two are in chronological order. Beyond that, the arrangement of the chapters becomes less significant since many of the topics address needs that may occur simultaneously, such as Motivation, Modifying Student Behaviour, and Developing Student Participation.

Some items from Day One and Day Two are interchangeable; for example, your school board may require you to send home your "Assessment and Evaluation Policy" on Day One instead of Day Two. It may be necessary to restructure the suggested timeline for the first two days and save some items for later in the week.

Do you have a difficult class and just bought this book mid-semester? Stop everything and make tomorrow your Day One. Focus on connecting with your students (see Tip 8). Be introspective. Ask yourself if you are modelling the behaviours you expect students to follow (see Tip 6). Accomplish these two things and you'll be back on track.

Don't be afraid to jump in anywhere and to modify any of the tips to suit your needs or those of your students.

I

PREPARATION STRATEGIES THAT PAY BIG DIVIDENDS

1. Get to Know Your Support Staff

Before the school year starts, introduce yourself to support staff, especially secretaries and custodians. Get to know their names and use them. Tell them that you are looking forward to working with them, and ask how their day is going. You want your interactions with them to be pleasant and run smoothly. Have a sense of humour; smile a lot and laugh often.

When opportunities arise, offer sincere compliments and congratulations. If a secretary or a custodian asks a favour, do it right away—when you're in a pinch, they will go the extra mile for you. Having their cooperation and support is vital.

2. Post Your Credentials

Take pride in your profession by posting your credentials. Doctors and lawyers post their diplomas and other credentials for all to see. This is a fine example of good public relations that teachers can easily mimic, especially if they have their own classroom.

You have worked long and hard at considerable financial expense just to be able to begin your career. The service you are providing is valuable. Display framed copies of your degrees and certificates including those from your ongoing professional development. This not only speaks to your credibility, but to your commitment to being a lifelong learner.

3. Preparing Your Classroom

Equipment Check

Advance preparation will go a long way toward providing an atmosphere that is conducive to learning. Make a list of improvements and repairs that are needed in your classroom. Complete and submit to the administration any required documentation and/or forms. The replacement of discoloured ceiling tiles and burned out light bulbs, and the need for repainting are just a few things to look for. Check electrical sockets for power, and make sure all necessary equipment is at hand and functioning properly. Be sure replacement bulbs for projectors are readily available. Adjust desks to take into account the location of all boards and viewing screens.

Visual Appearance

Put some thought into the overall appearance of your room. Strive to combine visual appeal with function. Decide where to post homework, special charts, word wall lists, and other visuals that you will need to access while teaching. Planning your layout ahead of time will help you achieve the desired result. Use your school colours as the basis for your bulletin boards.

Dare to be different. For example, in a geography class, run the lines of latitude and longitude that are closest to the location of your city, town, or school across your ceiling and label them appropriately. If painting them isn't an option, use construction paper, ribbon, or streamers. If you have a low ceiling, don't make it too distracting. In a math class, hang mobiles or 3D shapes along the back or sides of the room. Include specialty bulletin boards such as "Sabres In The News" (see Tip 61).

Hint: When hanging materials from the ceiling or walls, check with administration to be sure you are not in violation of safety regulations such as local fire codes.

4. The Photocopier: Your Lifeline

The increased use of iPads and other tablets has made the paperless classroom a reality for some; but, for the vast majority of teachers, the photocopier continues to be their lifeline. Knowing this, try to have all your photocopies run off no later than the day before they are needed. The one day you don't, Murphy's Law is sure to strike. A sick child at home or unforeseen traffic problems may cause you to arrive at work later than usual, only to find that the copier line up is long and the photocopiers in the staff room are jamming up. You can successfully navigate a situation like this with a little advance planning:

- Locate every copier in the school that is accessible to you.
- Be sure your access code works on each machine.
- Become familiar with their operation.
- Know how to troubleshoot common copier problems.

Hint: Since many schools limit your photocopies, run the exact number needed. Write the names of absent students on their copies. Place them in a special folder in your desk and distribute them when the students return. This minimizes the number of copies required and ensures that every student has one.

If you are unable to copy what you need for an instructional class, you can modify your lesson, but this should never happen on a test day. Many of your students will be ready and anxious to write, only to find that it is their teacher who is unprepared. Think of the message this sends your students. Photocopy tests at least a day ahead to avoid this embarrassing problem.

5. Relax and Be Yourself

I can't emphasize this one enough. Bring your own personality to the job! Knowing that you are thoroughly prepared inspires confidence, and you should be able to relax and be yourself. Most of us are familiar with late night talk show hosts Jimmy Fallon and Jimmy Kimmel. These outstanding comedians have both achieved a great deal, and each lends his own distinct personality to the job. Don't try to be someone you're not. If you are uncomfortable in your own skin, your students are sure to pick up on it.

II

DAY ONE—THE MOST
IMPORTANT DAY OF ALL

6. First Impressions:
Model, Model, Model

The first day of any class is most important, as it sets the tone and atmosphere for what is to come. In order to make a good first impression, model the following behaviours:

- Arrive early. This will allow you to get your day off to a smooth start.
- Be super organized. Double check that your classroom is neat and that everything you need for the day is at hand, including AV equipment, photocopies, and other materials.
- Post or display pertinent information, such as:
  - today's date and day of the cycle;
  - a welcome that includes your name, grade, and subject; and
  - specific seating instructions.
- Stand outside your classroom door to greet students with a smile and a friendly welcome.
- Begin promptly; any delay encourages distractions.
- Include something novel that sets you apart from other classes, e.g., projecting "Today's Quote," the seating plan, a puzzle, or a game from your laptop.
- Be enthusiastic (see Tip 9).
- Be respectful to all (see Tip 10).
- Know your subject material, school rules, and procedures inside out.

Most students are eager to please their teachers and will follow their lead. It is imperative that teachers consistently model the behaviours they expect from their students. A teacher who is organized and well prepared will project a great deal more confidence and appear to be in charge. Students are forever watching and this won't go unnoticed.

7. Use Announcements to Develop Listening Skills

Right from Day One, insist that students be quiet and attentive during announcements. Many of these messages may not pertain to individual students, so it is easy for their attention to wander. This can lead to misbehaviour. You'll need to develop a rationale with your class regarding the importance of listening to all announcements. If you involve them in the decision-making process, they are much more likely to be cooperative. Your class rationale may include:

- respecting others—although a certain announcement may not pertain to you, there may be others in the class who need to hear it;
- learning of opportunities to join clubs or school teams;
- hearing information about bursaries, university/college presentations, and career expositions;
- keeping abreast of what is going on in the school; and
- developing listening skills.

Suggested activity: once a week pre-read announcements that have been submitted early and make up a short quiz for your class. You may even want to submit an announcement of your own.

Encourage students to ask questions regarding announcements. Clarifying school policies or supplying additional information on upcoming activities is time well spent.

8. It's Time to Connect

On Day One, connecting with students should be your primary objective. Accomplish this and you will be well on your way to gaining their cooperation.

Before students enter your class, post your name on the board followed by a number that has some significance to you. This may start a discussion among some of your students even before class begins. At the sound of the bell shut your door, introduce yourself and ask your students what they think the number after your name stands for. It may represent the number of years you've been teaching, the number of schools you've taught at including supply and practice teaching, or the number of years of schooling you needed to reach this point. Students love to guess, and right away you've got them engaged. This serves as a perfect launch pad to tell them more about yourself without getting too personal. You may want to tell them about the schools you've attended, the sports or clubs you've been involved with at school, and the activities you plan to be part of this year. Extend an invitation for your students to join you in these activities. This process will humanize you and demonstrate your caring attitude. Finally, let them know that you love your job and are looking forward to working with them.

During the first week, have all students fill out a personal information form and an interest inventory including their involvement in sports, clubs, outdoor activities, church groups, and hobbies, and their favourite musical groups or performers. Try to remember at least one or two things that stand out about each individual. If you are able to bring up even one of these activities or interests in conversation outside the classroom then you'll have made quite an impression. You can take this to the next level by attending one of their events and it does not have to be school sponsored. Doing this will help you to connect with your students, especially those who seem hard to reach in the confines of the classroom.

9. Enthusiasm Is Infectious!

Show your students that you love what you do. Be passionate about the subjects you teach. Your actions will speak volumes (model, model, model), and your students will naturally become more attentive and engaged. One day, after one of my particularly enthusiastic presentations, a student responded with, "Gee, sir...that was intense!" Sensing an opportunity to have a little fun, I drew a quick sketch on the board of a couple of kids camping and said, "You see those two kids, they're *in tents*." The students had a good laugh and it provided a great segue into our next activity. Be ready to "bring it" every day.

10. Respect All Others (And Yourself)

You can't get away from rules, and none is more important than to respect all others, and yourself. This is the one rule that covers so many situations. For example, being late, not being prepared for class, being rude, interrupting and distracting others, making fun of classmates, and bullying are all forms of disrespect for the teacher and/or classmates. Be sure students understand, right from the beginning, that each one of them is important and has the right to be treated with respect. Any disrespectful behaviour will simply not be tolerated.

Ask your students what they think "self-respect" means. This can include such things as getting enough rest, exercise, or recreation, and having a good breakfast before school—maintaining balance in life is one of the trickiest things to achieve. Add to this the development of good work habits that will help bring success in school and other pursuits.

11. Choose Seating Plans Wisely

Seating plans are not a one-size-fits-all proposition and most teachers will employ a variety of seating plans throughout the years. Though you may have a preferred arrangement, seating may need to be adjusted depending on the curriculum, the classroom dynamics, your teaching style, and type of activities you have planned. For example, working in pairs or larger groups may necessitate the grouping of desks, and certain presentations may be best done using a theatre-type arrangement of seats. Preparing an appropriate seating arrangement for each activity is key to achieving a successful classroom dynamic. Most importantly, your choice of seating should facilitate, not impede, the flow of learning.

After a short time with your class, combine weaker and stronger students in homework pairs (see Tip 45). One year I had four Grade 12 boys in my Grade 11 math class. They asked if they could sit together, and promised to get their work done and not bother anyone else. The boys were very convincing and I had taught two of them before, so I decided to give it a try. They were fantastic. Not only did this foursome behave themselves, they worked very hard together as a group every day. I was really proud of these boys and they all earned very good grades.

There is nothing wrong with choosing alphabetical order for your seating plans. Letting students sit next to their best friends can be a way of inviting distractions. Shake things up a little by using reverse alphabetical order. Make it a practice to accommodate students who need a seat at the front of your room such as those with vision problems. To improve academic focus, members of our football teams were required by their coaches to request seats at the front of the room. Once you have dealt with these special circumstances, continue to seat remaining students alphabetically. As a bonus, I found that using alphabetical order facilitated learning students' names.

If students complain about these or any other arrangements, I suggest a response such as this: "You're doing really well where you are and I don't want to mess with success." Chances are the subject will not be broached again.

12. Learning Names Is a Priority

Students should be aware from Day One that their names are important to you. Not only does this show that you care about each and every student, but it also creates more positive interactions and helps lessons flow smoothly. Some teachers have a knack for committing names to memory; for the rest of us here are some helpful suggestions:

◆ Test yourself aloud in front of the whole class at the start and/or end of each period. If only a last name rings a bell, use it. For example, address them as "Mr. Mendez" or "Ms. Grainger." Do this daily until you have mastered all students' names.

- Use students' names during Q & A sessions, even if you have to carry a seating plan with you as you move about the room.
- Call on all students to answer—even those who don't raise their hands.
- Seat students in alphabetical order.
- Include student photos in your seating plans. This is extremely helpful to substitute teachers and colleagues who may have to cover your classes.
- Make sure students put their first and last names on everything they submit. Read their full names out loud when returning these items.
- Use students' names when you pass them in the hall. If you're struggling to remember a name, don't be afraid to stop and ask. Then, find a way to use it right away, such as, "Abdul, I really liked the way you volunteered answers today."

Avoid using nicknames such as "Mouse" for quiet students. Use of a student's actual name conveys respect and helps to maintain your professionalism (see Tip 34). Many students prefer teachers to use a less formal version of their name. For example, "Rick" or "Ricky" instead of "Richard" and there is no harm in doing that.

13. The Name Game

Here's a fun activity that can be used to set up your seating plan. Follow this procedure:

1. Call out the first name on your list and have the student go to the board and print his or her last name only, e.g., Atkinson.

2. Announce the score for the name (see Scoring Method, below), then ask the student to print the score after it (e.g., Atkinson 35) and direct him or her to a specific seat.

3. Students try to figure out how the names are being scored. When they think they know, they must raise their hands to give the score (e.g., Beaudoin 53).

4. If an incorrect answer is given, the teacher scores the name unless there are others with their hands up.

5. The first student to give a correct answer takes over the scoring from the teacher and is not allowed to tell anyone how it works.

6. Continue through the entire class, asking anyone who volunteers to score a name.

OPTION: Once two or more students have figured it out, ask them to find an algebraic expression to represent the score for any name. This keeps everybody engaged. Ask for this answer only after the entire class has been scored and seated.

Scoring Method: Vowels are worth 10 points and consonants are worth one. Atkinson has three vowels worth 30 points and five consonants worth five points. Add to get 35 points. More simply, the number of vowels goes first, followed by the number of consonants.

Hints:

* Short names are much easier to score, e.g., Azar 22 and Wong 13.

◆ 10x + y is an algebraic expression that can be used to score any name, where x represents the number of vowels and y the number of consonants.

WARNING: The letter y is sometimes a vowel and sometimes a consonant. This can cause confusion, but it simply adds to the fun. For example, Yaworsky—the first y is a consonant and the last is a vowel, making Yaworsky worth 35. Pretty cool!

With a little effort many mundane tasks, such as seating students, can be turned into activities your classes are sure to enjoy. When my daughter, a high school English teacher, was married her name changed from Gomes to Fazio altering her score from 23 to 32. My usual joke is that she lost a consonant but gained a vowel.

14. Avoid Power Struggles

Avoid making comments such as, "The moment you enter this door, I'm in charge." Many students will take offence to such heavy-handed statements and react negatively and power struggles are bound to begin. While teachers need to be in control of their classes, there is no need to try to establish authority in such a confrontational way.

Let your actions speak louder than your words. Model the behaviours that you expect students to emulate. Being super organized, respectful, knowledgeable, and enthusiastic will go a long way toward establishing your credibility and students will see that you are indeed in charge.

15. What to Send Home on Day One

Send students home with any first day information sheets to be read and signed by a parent and returned the following day. Getting students to return signed forms can be a real headache. To make things run more smoothly, have a discussion about the importance of being responsible. Let your students know that getting these forms back promptly is very important to you, and that you do not want to waste valuable time chasing down these forms and assigning consequences. Tell them that you do not enjoy doling out consequences and seeing students spend their valuable time dealing with the fallout. Make students aware of the consequences for not turning in the signed forms on time. I have found that discussing responsibility and presenting consequences not as punishment, but as an incentive to get the job done, has two dramatic benefits. First, the number of students who are late turning in their forms is minimal. Second, being forewarned, the students complied with the assigned consequences without complaint.

Hints:

- When sending anything home to parents via the student, include this responsibility on your "Homework Board" (see Tip 46) and have students copy the required action such as "Get English test signed" into their agendas (see Tip 20).
- Any consequences that you assign should be reasonable, have the support of administration, and be self-administered.
- Some teachers develop their own rewards program for students who turn things in promptly.

It is crucial that teachers set up a system to track student compliance and follow through with consequences when necessary. I used to require my high school students to submit a handwritten copy of the forms that had not been signed and returned on time. An extra day was given to hand in these copies along with the original signed forms.

Keep Day One's homework brief, and be sure it's worthwhile. Possible activities for students include:

- clipping newspaper or magazine ads or pictures to decorate bulletin boards;
- printing off a times table grid from the Internet, highlighting the answers they know, and learning five new products for tomorrow;
- writing a 150-word paragraph about something related to a specific topic; and
- completing a puzzle related to an upcoming lesson.

Remind your students that first impressions are very important and that you will be checking their homework regularly and tracking it.

16. Late Policy: An Essential Component

At most schools, a student who arrives late for the start of the school day is required to sign in at the office before going to class. These lates are tracked and often dealt with by the school administration. Throughout the school day, and especially if students are on a rotary timetable, other lates will occur. It is essential that teachers, as well as the main office, have a classroom late policy in place and that they are consistent in its application.

Don't leave your students in the dark. Have a brief Q & A with your class about the importance of being on time. Then cover the key elements of your late policy. Inform students that they are expected to be on time, with their materials in hand. Arriving before the bell and asking to go to your locker to get your things still constitutes a late. As I would often say to my classes, "A carpenter can't go to work without his tools." Students respect such real-life examples because they can relate to them.

My door was closed and locked on the bell. Students who arrived late would knock and often had to wait quietly for a minute or two until any class discussion ended. Once allowed in, students would sign the late sheet on the corner of my desk, indicate their time of arrival, and then take their seats. Later in the period, I would stop by their desks and query them about their lates. If the late was not excused, the student would be given a late form to complete for the next day that included:

- the student's name, date, and time of arrival;
- the reason for being late;
- a paragraph explaining the importance of being on time;
- a paragraph outlining a plan to avoid being late again; and
- the student's signature.

Be sure that late students know you are recording their names in your daybook and that you expect each of them to submit a properly completed handwritten form for the next day. Remind students that you will be reading their forms carefully before discussing their responses with them. Whatever your policy, consistent follow up is a must.

17. Dismissing Students

Don't allow your students to pack up early and pile up at the door awaiting the bell. As teachers, we are preparing our students for their future and we should send the message that the limited time we have with them is valuable and not to be wasted. Check that the clock in your room is in sync with the one in the main office. Make it a practice to keep your students working until just a few seconds before the bell, unless you have any last-minute instructions you need to share with them. Do your best to dismiss them on time; however, they must understand that it is the teacher who dismisses them, not the bell. Likewise, teachers must not let their classes out early as this not only disturbs other classes in session but also puts pressure on other teachers to do the same.

Remind students not to leave any items behind. I often ended class by saying, "Don't leave me any presents." The first few days of school and test days seem to be the worst in this regard. If textbooks or eyeglasses were left behind, I would try to return the item(s) to the student during my prep or lunch periods. Another option is to have the student paged to the office to pick up the item(s). Although teachers should encourage "taking responsibility," they should weigh it against the importance of demonstrating kindness.

III

DAY TWO—CLARIFYING POLICIES AND PROCEDURES

18. Spell Out Student Responsibilities

Establish a routine for students to follow each day upon arrival in your classroom. Students must be prepared for the moment that the teacher is ready to begin the class. These requirements may vary from teacher to teacher, but such routines are lifesavers.

Expect them to sit in their usual seats and open their books to the last day's work. This provides an orderly atmosphere in which to address the class as a whole, even if they are continuing to work in the same groups they were in the previous day.

You may need to remind your students of their responsibilities for the first week. Instead of harping on expected behaviours, praise a student who is in compliance. For example, "Carson, I couldn't help but notice that as soon you sat down, you put things away, then opened your notebook to your homework and placed your pencil and eraser on your desk. That's what I like to see." Use praise instead of criticism.

19. Washroom Policy: Limit Your Headaches

School administration may have developed a washroom policy that works efficiently. You may need to tweak it, or if none exists, develop a washroom policy of your own. It should make students accountable, require little effort on your part, minimize interruption to the learning environment, and maintain some degree of flexibility.

Students should make every effort to use the washroom outside of instructional time. If not, have students follow these procedures:

- Come to class first and ask permission to sign out before going to the washroom. Students should not show up late for class and use the excuse that they were in the washroom, except in extenuating circumstances.
- Use the nearest washroom when leaving the classroom.
- Avoid asking to use the washroom while the teacher is instructing. It's deadly when you reach the crux of your lesson and call on Suzie, only to have her ask to use the washroom.
- Let the teacher know if they are feeling ill when asking to use the washroom.

> **Hint:** When my students asked permission to use the washroom I would often reply, "Not right now," if I felt it was bad timing or that they were trying to abuse this privilege. Often, they would not ask again for the remainder of the period.

A student who has left the room during your class is still your responsibility. If a student has not returned from the washroom after a reasonable amount of time, send a classmate to check on him or her. The student may have passed out in the washroom or become ill and require assistance. It is easy to get wrapped up in your lesson and forget that one of your students is out of the room.

Hints:

- As a precaution, many elementary schools require younger students to go to the washroom in pairs.

- Check with the administration to determine in advance how to handle emergency situations such as students who have gone to the washroom during fire drills, severe weather alerts, or lockdowns.
- Have students who have been granted permission to use the washroom print their names on a designated area of the board including a sign-out/sign-in time. This serves as a visual reminder to the teacher that someone is out of the room and reinforces to the entire class that their time management is being monitored.

20. Homework Policy and Guidelines

It is no surprise that students who complete homework regularly will find it easier to prepare for tests than those who neglect their homework and try to cram it all in at the last minute. Use the following adage to illustrate this point and discuss it with your students: "Inch by inch, life's a cinch. Yard by yard, life's hard." Then lay out your homework policy:

- Homework will be assigned daily.
- It is due the next day at the start of class.
- Homework completion will be checked and recorded frequently.
- Parents will be contacted if students are not completing homework. (This is not designed to get students in trouble, but to assist them in achieving success.)

Homework Guidelines:

- Stay within the parameters of the homework policy developed by school board administration.

- Have a system in place for students to record their homework. Many schools provide students with personal agendas that can be used for this purpose.
- Vary the intensity, duration, and type of homework.
- Give students an opportunity to solve incomplete homework issues on their own prior to parental involvement.

Anything you can do to lighten the mood when assigning homework will make the task more enjoyable for your students. Sometimes when assigning homework, I would draw a pentagon on the board that looked like the profile of a house. I even added a chimney or a door for those students who didn't catch on. Then, I would write the day's homework inside the house.

21. Assessment and Evaluation Policy

Provide your students and their parents with a list of assessment instruments that will be used throughout the course. This list should include information about the scheduling of major tests, assignments and projects, as well as the relative weighting of these evaluations. The weighting of term work as compared to the final exam or any final summative assessment, if there is one, is another important consideration. Be transparent—where age appropriate, provide students with a marks record sheet for recording and calculating their marks. This eliminates the problem of students continually asking for their grades.

Do all you can to limit student absence on test days (see Tip 90) but as hard as you try, some students may still be absent. Now you've got to take care of the details. Who gets a make-up test? When and where will it be written? If eligible, students writing make-ups should be properly supervised, either by yourself or one of your peers.

Provide parents with a copy of your make-up test policy. Our department, supported by school administration, allowed a student to be absent for one test without a doctor's note. Any subsequent test that was missed would require a formal doctor's note before scheduling a make-up. In most cases, extended absences being one exception, students should write make-up tests on the day they return to class.

> **Hint:** It is a good idea to share your policy with school administration and obtain their support prior to its distribution.

For whatever policy you adopt, make sure that it is put in writing and that parents have read, signed, and returned it to you.

22. Maintain a Degree of Flexibility

In most cases you'll be able to follow the rules that you have established. But taking a cookie cutter approach to problems that arise isn't always fair or reasonable. Once a parent called me on a test day regarding her son's absence. This was the second time he missed a test and a doctor's note would normally be required. Well, the poor boy was quite sick and she didn't have a car to take him to the doctor. Besides, they were having trouble making ends meet and she couldn't afford the money for the doctor's note and a cab. I simply thanked her for calling, told her not to worry about the note, asked her to tell her son to focus on getting well, and said he could write his test when he returned. Sometimes rules may need to be broken—or at least bent!

23. Establish Guidelines for Known Absentees

Be proactive by informing students that once they are aware of an upcoming absence, they should notify the teacher immediately. Assist them in developing an action plan with the goal of minimizing or eliminating the effect of an absence. This may involve having a student work ahead or arrange for some tutoring. As well, students should expect to complete some classwork while on a family vacation or an extended school field trip. Oftentimes, students will work together on the bus, especially if the trips are quite long. In the case of overnight trips, the staff in charge may set aside a daily study period. Students on these trips tend to bond and often form study groups. Contacting the teacher supervisor prior to extended field trips is always a good idea.

I have had students who returned to their homeland with parents or who entered hospital for major surgeries and as a result, missed half a semester. In some cases, the school board was able to provide in-home tutoring, and I would photocopy notes from one of my top students for the absentees. Many times homework for the week would be bundled up and sent to me for review, comment, and grading. Though it often required a fair amount of extra work, helping these students to be successful made it worthwhile.

24. Be Approachable

Provide parents with your contact information and times when you can be reached. Inform both parents and students of your availability for extra help. This sends a clear message that you are both approachable and concerned about student success.

As previously mentioned, it is vital that you connect with your students, preferably on Day One. If students know that you are fully invested in them, then you will have earned their respect, trust, and cooperation. They will see you as a teacher who is approachable, not just an authority figure. As a result, students will be more apt to approach you to get the help they need. If you sense that a student is worried about something, strike up a conversation to see if the problem surfaces on its own. If not, tell the student that you are concerned. Then listen.

It is important to let students know your schedule. During the day, you may be teaching in more than one classroom and after school you may be difficult to find due to staff meetings, extra help sessions, and extracurricular commitments. When I was coaching a school team, I found it especially advantageous to have a printout of every player's schedule and for team members to know mine. Unforeseen circumstances, ranging from a player coming down with the flu to a sudden death in the family, will inevitably arise, and you should be prepared for such contingencies.

IV

INFLUENCING AND MODIFYING STUDENT BEHAVIOUR

25. Use Nonverbal Cues

Nonverbal cues can effectively influence student behaviour. You can keep the ball rolling, with little or no interruption to your lesson or activity, by using nonverbal cues such as those listed below:

- Make eye contact. A good stare combined with an appropriate facial expression, such as a raised eyebrow, can abruptly terminate an unwanted behaviour.
- Use the "zip it" gesture as if pulling a zipper shut across the lips to request silence.
- As soon as you see a student attempting to distract another, write his name on the board, e.g., Paul. If he doesn't notice, someone else will bring it to his attention quickly. If he raises his hand, do not call on him. Simply state, "Paul, we'll discuss what this means later," and move on.
- If you notice students working in a group watching you, make a rolling circular motion with one hand; this will send a message to "get on with it."
- If students are watching you during a test, quickly take two fingers and point them toward your own eyes then tap your fingers gently on the nearest desk. This should send a clear message to students about keeping focused on their own work.
- Baseball coaches are masters of nonverbal communication. Follow their lead and develop signs of your own, e.g., wiping your forehead, stroking your chin, adjusting your tie, and pulling on your ear lobe.

The list above mainly focuses on deterring undesirable behaviours. Nonverbal communication, such as the wink of an

eye, the nod of the head, or thumbs up can be used to rein-
force positive behaviours as well. Letting students know you
are pleased with their work or behaviour should always be
a priority.

26. Nip It in the Bud with Name Recognition

When a student's attention begins to wander while you are
talking to the class, simply insert his or her name into your
sentence, e.g., "Marks will be deducted, Jake, for bad form."
Merely the sound of his name is usually enough to bring Jake
back on task without impeding the flow of your lesson.

This situation underscores the importance of learning every
student's name as soon as possible. It would be difficult to
employ this technique effectively without knowing Jake's
name, and you certainly wouldn't want to refer to him as "you
at the back."

27. Use Space to Your Advantage

Use proximity to your advantage. If a student begins to write
a note or engage in distracting behaviour, you may not have
to say a word. Walk toward the vicinity of the student as you
continue to address the class as a whole. If the behaviour
ceases, stop briefly to ensure that it isn't going to continue; if
not, keep moving closer. You may even want to stand next to
the student's desk for a moment for emphasis or between two
parties attempting to converse. Closing in on personal space
can stop unwanted behaviour dead in its tracks.

Hint: It is important that teachers don't spend all of their time at the front of the room. Moving about the classroom when instructing sends a signal to all students that they are important to you. This easy-to-use technique helps keep students engaged in the learning process.

28. Be Firm but Fair

Being firm requires you to be consistent in dealing with disrespectful behaviours. Don't let things slide. Ignoring unacceptable classroom behaviour, especially the kind that is hurtful to others, will only result in such instances increasing in frequency, intensity, and duration. Like a snowball rolling down a hill, it creates its own momentum.

Achieving fairness is an ideal we should all strive for, and I think we'd all agree that the consequences should "fit the crime." In fact, being fair to one another is part of our primary rule, "Respect all others." However, being fair does not always mean treating everyone the same, as in the case of a repeat offender versus the first-time offender. You may also find that certain consequences are ineffective with an individual student and you may have to try something different.

From time to time, a student may complain about being treated unfairly. It's common to hear, "That's not fair, sir. I wasn't the only one talking." When this occurred in my classroom, I would reply, "That may be so, but a cop doesn't catch all the speeders." (Students love such common sense. Real-life analogies almost always put a halt to any rebuttal.) They learn that just because others may not have been caught, this does not excuse their inappropriate behaviour.

29. Getting a Student Back on Track

It's not uncommon for a student to lose focus and when this happens, your goal is to get the student engaged as quickly as possible. Let's assume one of your pupils has become distracted. Simply ask that individual to read something to the class from a readily available source, such as a classroom poster or notes on the board.

When attempting to modify a student's behaviour in front of the class, follow a few simple rules:

 • Be calm and respectful. You may need to raise, lower, or change the inflection of your voice, but don't shout.
 • Keep the focus on returning to appropriate behaviour, not the distraction.
 • Avoid asking questions.
 • Keep your requests short and to the point.
 • Repeat the instructions, if necessary.
 • Avoid arguing. Do not let the classroom become the student's forum.

Getting a student refocused does not have to be difficult, but like a good puppet master you must pull all the right strings.

30. Avoid Escalation: Be Careful What You Ask

In most cases, do not ask questions of misbehaving students in front of the class. This often leads to situations where students try to save face in the presence of their peers, regardless of the long-term consequences. The results can be devastating.

If you choose to query students in front of their peers, follow the tried-and-true maxim from law school: never ask a question you don't already know the answer to. For example, upon noticing Earl goofing around, Mrs. Johnson inquired, "Earl are you having fun?" Talk about leaving yourself open for a broadside. At first glance, this may seem to invite a simple yes or no answer. But, Earl replied, "Not as much fun as I had with my girlfriend last night." The result, of course, was uproar in the class that turned into an embarrassing moment for the teacher. Her response to this unexpected reply could exacerbate an already bad situation and spiral the class out of control. More importantly, this leads to a loss of respect for the teacher.

31. When Consequences Are Necessary

Undesirable behaviour need not always result in a consequence for the student. As we have seen, good teachers employ a variety of tools and strategies to put a quick stop to unwanted behaviours and re-engage students with little or no interruption to the flow of their lesson.

More serious breaches to the class/school code of conduct should be dealt with promptly. It is important that teachers maintain their composure and be respectful even when dealing with a misbehaving student. Your goal should be to put an end to the unwanted behaviour and get the student re-engaged in the learning process as soon as possible. The assigning of consequences should be dealt with one-on-one (see Tip 32), and later in the period, to avoid adding fuel to the fire.

Consider the following scenario: Kyle throws a paper airplane across the room. Many of the students begin to laugh. You ask him to pick up the plane and place it in the garbage can. He complies, but puts on a performance in doing so. This draws a few more laughs. If you choose to speak again, say something brief and to the point, such as, "Kyle, please return to your seat." You may not, however, need to say another word. A simple stare combined with a look of disbelief may be all that is needed. In either case, as Kyle returns to his seat record his name and assign a consequence later.

In doling out the consequence, you could use simple multiplication. If the entire process took about half a minute and there are 30 people in the class, then Kyle owes you 0.5 x 30 = 15 minutes. Next, you must decide on the consequence itself. It could simply be a 15-minute detention or student-teacher conference (see Tip 33), or you may attempt to link the punishment to the crime. For example, you could have Kyle complete a writing assignment dealing with what makes a good design for a paper airplane or what gives a real airplane lift. Insist that the report is handwritten and include specifics such as, one full page, no skipping lines, paragraph form, and due prior to the start of class tomorrow. Another possibility is to try metacognitive reflection. Create a simple form for the student to complete including:

- the student's name, date, and period number;
- a description of student's actions;
- an explanation of why he or she behaved this way;
- identifying problems caused by the student's behaviour;
- an explanation of how the student plans to avoid such behaviour from occurring again; and
- the student's signature.

Before he completes the form, make sure Kyle knows you will be reviewing it with him and that he may need to make improvements to his responses. Keep the form in a file for future reference. For very young students, a simple apology note may suffice.

32. One-on-One

Dealing with a problem one-on-one gives you much more control over the situation. Depending on the circumstances, it may be best to ask a misbehaving student to step into the hall for a moment. You don't have to worry about interruptions from other students who may want to come to their classmate's rescue, and at the same time you haven't let the classroom become the offending student's forum.

> **Hint:** Ensure the other students have something constructive to do while you are in the hall. Idle time is your enemy!

Consider the case of Kyle from the previous tip. Let's assume that you asked Kyle to take his seat after his little performance and he muttered something rude that you were able to hear. Ask Kyle to step out into the hall. Do not start the conversation by taking a combative stance. Instead, start with something positive, such as, "Kyle, I enjoy having you in my class and I think you have a lot of potential. I really would like to help you be successful. Is there something you would like to tell me that caused you to behave this way?" Then pause and listen. Next, let Kyle know you are disappointed in his actions and you expect better of him. Refer to how his disrespectful behaviour has negatively impacted the learning process. Let him know that it's important for him to focus on the day's work and that you will discuss his consequences with him later. Shortly after you resume your lesson or activity, try to get Kyle involved by asking him to respond to a question or to read something to the class. Then provide some positive feedback such as, "Well done, Kyle." By dealing with Kyle in a respectful manner and showing concern for him, you are much more likely to achieve the desired result and less likely to have future problems with him.

33. Structure Your Consequences

Students should be made aware of the consequences of disrespectful behaviour. These consequences should be structured to follow the concepts below:

- The punishment should fit the crime—the greater the infraction, the greater the consequence.
- Different consequences may be required for different students.
- Repeat offenders will be dealt with more severely than first-time offenders. For example, completion of the late form for the next day may suffice for the first unexcused late. Upon reaching three unexcused lates, a 15-minute student-teacher conference may be added to the completion of the late form.

> **Hint:** Avoid the use of the word "detention." The word "conference" helps to frame things in a more positive light. The whole point of the meeting is to resolve the problem. If the conference does not last for the allotted time, the student can stay and complete some homework.

Don't get caught developing your consequences as you go—be proactive. Make a list of common behavioural issues you are likely to face, along with a corresponding set of consequences.

Do this and your chances of being caught off guard will be significantly reduced.

34. Maintain Your Professionalism

Remember, you are first and foremost a student's teacher and you must maintain your professionalism.

Having entered the teaching profession, I hope you are a social person who enjoys working with young people. I truly don't know of a teacher who doesn't want to be liked by students. It is a big mistake, however, to try to become their friend. This can lead to a whole host of problems—conflict of interest and other allegations of misconduct. Your focus should be on providing your students with a safe, respectful, and intellectually stimulating environment in which to learn. Accomplish this and you will have their respect and appreciation for a job well done.

35. Call on Your Colleagues

If you are uncomfortable with how you've handled a situation involving a student, consult one or more of your colleagues. You are bound to gain new insights into the problem. If you are lucky, the first person you consult will offer a solution you are happy with, but in most cases, you will need to acquire several opinions before you find an appropriate solution. Quite often, you will create your own solution by combining advice from several of your colleagues. Drawing on their varied experiences is not only a useful tool, but it also lets them know that you value their opinions.

36. Sending a Student to the Office Is Your Last Resort

Maximizing learning by minimizing the number of behavioural issues should be every teacher's goal. Good teachers handle almost all of their own discipline and send students to the office only as a last resort.

Some teachers struggle with classroom management day after day, yet others seem to glide along with only occasional problems. Teachers in the latter group manage their classrooms in such a way that behavioural disruptions are infrequent. Connecting with their students; being respectful, enthusiastic and knowledgeable; providing well organized and engaging lessons; and having effective rules and procedures in place are all keys to this end.

Do not send a student to the office for a frivolous reason, such as not having a pencil. When undesirable behaviours do occur, a good teacher will be able to stop almost all of them from escalating to the point where office intervention becomes necessary (see Tips 25-35). However, certain instances, such as physical threats directed toward a teacher or a student may require office intervention and immediate removal of the student from the room.

Teachers who seldom send students to the office convey the message that they have good classroom management skills. Consequently, their requests for effective office intervention, when required, will be taken more seriously.

37. A Student's Successful Return to Class

A student should only be sent to the office for a serious matter. That student should not be allowed to rejoin the class until you have had a chance to discuss the situation with the person in charge, and preferably with the student as well. It is incumbent upon the teacher to follow up with whoever is handling this matter, usually the principal or vice-principal. If you can't get to see this person in a timely fashion, send an e-mail requesting an after-school meeting. If it can't be scheduled at the end of the day, request a meeting prior to school the next day. You want to get the matter resolved and pave the way for the student's successful transition back into your classroom.

It is beneficial to meet with the student prior to his or her return. A frank discussion about the issue, requirements for rejoining the class, and your expectations upon return can go a long way toward avoiding further problems. This meeting between the student and teacher may also include the parents, an administrator, and other resource people from the school staff. Be sure to come to the meeting prepared with any pertinent information and have some helpful suggestions for facilitating the student's return to your classroom.

> **Hint:** At some point in the process, usually in private, the principal or vice-principal may offer suggestions on how you could have handled the situation differently. Keep an open mind. This may provide a real opportunity to improve your classroom management skills.

38. Going Above and Beyond

Perhaps the greatest gift you can give as a teacher is the gift of time. Students respond positively to teachers who go above and beyond the call of duty. These students are generally appreciative and show improved participation in their classes.

When you stay on a Friday after school with a struggling student for an extra hour, it shows how much you care. When you take time to write comments on assignments and tests, it shows that you care. When you call parents during evenings and weekends to help get students on track, it shows you care. When you devote your time to extra curricular activities, it shows you care. When you attend athletic events, performances and other activities your students are involved in, whether a school activity or not, it shows you care. These are only a few of the many ways teachers touch the lives of their students by showing they care. In the end, education is much more about people than it is about subject content. Touch the lives of children by instilling self-confidence and inspiration—then watch them soar!

39. Extracurricular Involvement

Teachers can extend their radius of influence a great deal by getting involved with students outside the classroom setting. Most coaches, for example, really want to impart life skills to their players, a loftier goal than just winning or losing. Teamwork is an essential component to the success of any group activity, and the bonds formed from the many hours spent working together for a common cause may last a lifetime. As a result, students usually have a great deal of respect for their coaches. This yields benefits to the teacher-coach in the classroom as well. Not only are students more apt to cause fewer discipline problems, they are more likely to increase their levels of participation in class. A positive ripple effect will occur, as many students who do not belong to your team or club will recognize the contributions you make to their friends, peers, and school as a whole.

40. Prepping Classes for Your Absence

Students appreciate teachers setting expectations and limits. When I knew in advance that I would be absent, I would always prep my classes by laying out my expectations and reminders as follows:

+ Be on time and sit in the proper seat.
+ Give the substitute your full cooperation.
+ Follow our usual protocols for cleaning the boards, distributing materials, and assisting with equipment.
+ Students whose names appear on the substitute's report for poor behaviour will be dealt with more severely than usual.
+ Problems reflect poorly on the student(s) involved, upon me, and upon our school.

Most often, I would receive glowing reports from my substitutes, and if there were any issues, I made sure to follow through with them.

41. What to Leave Your Substitute

If you want students to take the work seriously, provide a relevant task that they will find meaningful. Create a separate folder for each class that contains:

- an accurate seating plan (preferably a photo seating plan);
- provisions for students with special needs and appropriate accommodations;
- a list of potentially disruptive students and information on what to look out for and possible solutions;
- attendance procedures to be followed;
- work to be assigned, e.g., readings, questions, and/or puzzles to be completed for the next day;
- a sufficient number of handouts for assigned work; and
- additional work for students who may finish early—the biggest problem for the substitute and for you occurs when insufficient work is left.

> **Hint:** I used to write my lessons below the seating plan or on the back of the same page. Fewer papers mean less chance of things getting lost.

In many cases, you may be getting a substitute teacher who will not have the expertise required in your subject area. Do not expect them to teach a formal lesson. Instead, let students do seat work. If the work you provide is mostly review, spice it up by including a puzzle. Some students will find it difficult to remain focused for the entire period, so providing some variety is important. Also, there are many guided learning or discovery exercises that they can attempt on their own. Your students can be left articles on related subject matter to read and answer questions. These are just a few appropriate ways to take the burden off the substitute teacher. If one of your peers is assigned to cover for you and is well qualified, ask about preferences. You might find he or she will welcome an opportunity to teach a different group of students.

V

CLASSROOM ROUTINES ARE CRITICAL

42. Time is Precious: Develop Efficient Routines

The development of efficient routines is critical to successful time management. Sloppy routines not only waste time, but they reflect poorly on the teacher. Though time is precious, your efforts will be rewarded tenfold with much improved classroom dynamics. Efficient routines do not stifle creativity; to the contrary, they provide a framework within which students can blossom.

Cleaning boards may seem like a minor matter, but my boards needed cleaning hundreds of times. Consequently, I developed a routine that almost ran itself and freed me up for more important tasks. My room had five rows of desks, each row named for a specific weekday. On a Tuesday, students from the "Tuesday" row would clean the boards as soon as they entered the room. If they forgot, I would say, "Tuesday row" and they would hop to it. When I noticed any shoddy work, I would say in a fun-loving way, "You know, they say good help is hard to find." If your classroom has more than five rows, be creative.

Unless you have a small class with only a few students in each row, don't ask students to "pass things back" as it is an inefficient method of distributing materials. For instance, it takes only one person in a row to drop the papers or not be paying attention to slow down or stop the process entirely. Instead, designate the first person in each row to perform this task. If you have two pages to distribute, give the second page to the second person in each row. If a large number of pages are to be given out and they are not stapled booklet style, then lay these out in order and have students pick them up a row at a time, or select a different student to pass out each page to the entire class.

43. Putting Student Work on the Board

In both math and geography classes, I regularly asked students to put work on the board and explain their solutions to the class when requested. Doing so helped develop their confidence and presentation skills. When students put work on the board, I usually followed the routine outlined below:

- Arrange question numbers on the board.
- Vary the student selection process, e.g., everybody in the Monday and Tuesday row.
- Ask for volunteers. To include some students who don't usually volunteer, randomly select, for example, the third person in each row.
- Have students print their first and last name next to their solution or answer.
- If homework is incomplete, students must still place their name and the question on the board. You can help them work their way through it if they seem completely stuck, but avoid giving them the solutions (see Tip 52).

It's a good idea to use a checklist to track student participation. Later, while students are working at their seats, note the names of those who were volunteering answers and adding to class discussions, and note others who may have had trouble explaining their problem-solving process.

44. Checking Homework

Homework completion is a primary concern to most parents. When checking homework, try the following strategies:

- Provide extra questions for students to attempt while you're checking homework.
- Include a challenge question.
- Check and track the homework of students who will be placing their work on the board first and then do the same for remaining students.
- Initial each student's homework. Include a code letter such as S or U for "satisfactory" or "unsatisfactory."
- Visit students at their desks or have them bring their work to you.

Hint: If you choose to have students bring you their work, allow only two or three students at a time to line up at your desk. As students sit down they are replaced by the next one in their row. Experiment to find out what works best for you.

Checking homework frequently and keeping accurate records is essential for all concerned. In addition, the simple process of initialling serves as an effective feedback mechanism for concerned parents.

45. Helping Each Other in Homework Pairs

Homework pairs is a quick and effective way to encourage student collaboration. You may want to employ this technique when you feel somewhat familiar with your students. To make the partner selection process easier and increase the effectiveness of your pairings, follow a few simple procedures:

- Ensure that every student has a homework partner.
- Say the command "homework pairs" and include a time restriction such as 5 or 10 minutes. Watch as your students put their desks together and begin reviewing homework difficulties.
- Have students who finish early put homework solutions on the board for a whole class discussion or assign them a challenge question to attempt.

Homework pairs is a convenient method of engaging students in the learning process right at the start of class. Students find this activity both academically beneficial and enjoyable.

46. The Homework Board as a Routine for the Teacher

Establish a set location where homework will be posted daily. Upcoming test dates and assignment due dates should appear on the homework board as well.

Often, students who were absent from class have come to my room later in the day to copy assigned work from the homework board. These students should be able to help themselves to the day's handouts, unless they are being kept in your desk or file cabinet. When siblings or friends of absent students show up looking for an absentee's homework, supply them with any required handouts and direct their attention to the homework board.

Such interruptions are commonplace in a teacher's day and their effects can be mitigated by having well-designed procedures in place.

VI

GRABBING YOUR STUDENTS' ATTENTION

47. Bell Work: Get 'er Done

Many teachers use bell work as an effective classroom management tool. It gets students on task quickly and frees up the teacher to complete other duties or assist students as required. More importantly, bell work can be used to improve fundamental skills. Increasing students' numeracy skills will be a great asset when it comes time for tackling algebra, just as improving their proficiency with literacy skills will make them better communicators.

Some teachers have their students start bell work the moment they enter the classroom and others prefer to begin on the bell. I like to give students a little down time during class change, but they must be ready to start at the sound of the bell. If you have a particularly challenging group of students, you may find the sooner they start the better.

Bell work should be short and timed. It can include drill-type questions of any kind. Try minute math, where students see how many correct answers they can complete in one minute. In chemistry, it could be identifying the correct compound, e.g., H_2O (water) or $CaCO_3$ (calcium carbonate or chalk). For language arts, you could ask students to fill in the blanks with the correct verb tense or proper homonym. Another popular choice is to have students use each word provided in a sentence. Regardless of the subject or question type, always take up the answers. This will provide valuable feedback to student and teacher alike, and may result in the teacher modifying the current day's lesson.

48. Increase Focus Using Video Clips

The Internet is loaded with free, attention-grabbing videos that are not only educational, but also quite often humorous. A vast array of videos is available on almost any topic. You will have to decide where a video fits best into your lesson, as these clips can be used in a variety of ways, such as an introduction, a writing prompt, a transition, a review, or a summation. Preview the entire video to make sure it is relevant to your lesson and the content is appropriate for your class. A colleague from another school once told me that he showed a film on Scandinavia that he had not previewed completely. Imagine his surprise when a few people exited a sauna entirely in the buff and began rolling around in the snow, as is their custom.

Have your students surf the Internet and submit suitable videos on upcoming topics. Provide guidelines as to their length and content. This saves you time and gets the students invested in their own learning. Review these videos and select the ones that are most beneficial, i.e., meet the expectations, for your lessons.

Want to get creative? Have your students make their own video clips. Divide your students into small groups and provide them with a list of topics complete with expectations. Together, discuss what makes an effective video. Supply guidelines including: an appropriate title, amount of running time, credits (to illustrate their roles), in-class time allotment, and due date. As an added bonus, having students make their own videos can address all learning styles (visual, auditory, and kinesthetic). Showing a couple of student-made videos that meet your expectations is the best way to get the results you desire.

49. Use Technology to Tap into Your Students' World

Technology provides us with a way to reach into the world of the 21st century student. As educators, we must be careful not to throw the baby out with the bathwater, but at the same time we should embrace new technologies as they can improve student engagement in the learning process. I believe we can benefit from the words of former *Chicago Sun-Times* financial analyst Robert P. Vanderpoel: "The most successful business-man is the man who holds onto the old as long as it is good, and grabs the new just as soon as it is better."

Use technologies such as interactive whiteboards (IWBs), tablets, student response systems, or even students' personal devices, if allowed, to enhance your teaching and student learning. Not only do these technologies offer outstanding visuals, but they also provide a great deal of flexibility, such as instant enlargement of diagrams and graphs. IWBs can be used to create dynamic and interactive lessons for students. With the use of tablets, you are able to redefine how students can show their learning by means of audio recordings and video and e-book creations.

50. Quotations, Puzzles, and Problem Solving

Post a quotation on the board or project one from your tablet, e.g., "Your attitude, not your aptitude, will determine your altitude" (Zig Ziglar). Allow students a couple of minutes to write about what the quote means to them and then follow up with discussion.

Have students work on a puzzle for a limited amount of time and then investigate the strategies they used to solve it. One of my favourites for math is a KenKen puzzle, which appears in many daily newspapers and is available on the Internet as well. The beauty of KenKen is that it combines basic math operations with problem-solving skills. The puzzles start with a 3x3 grid, and I've seen them as large as 9x9 and at various levels of difficulty.

Hint: Post two puzzles at different levels of difficulty to provide encouragement for students with varied abilities.

51. Grasp Teachable Moments When Opportunity Knocks

Sometimes you can prepare for the teachable moment in advance, but you'll be surprised how often these opportunities arise out of the blue. When opportunity knocks, answer! A few examples are listed below:

- The equinox only happens twice a year, during March and September. Incorporate these special events into your lessons. Use Google to find poems for the vernal and autumnal equinox.
- When your first late student arrives in class, use this opportunity to review late procedures.
- The day after calling a number of parents, tell students you enjoyed speaking with their parents and discussing action plans for student success. Present this positively to the entire class.

In my last year of teaching, a unique unexpected teachable moment arose. A student in my Grade 9 math class placed a square root symbol on the board around his name, which just happened to be Raad (pronounced Rad). I have no idea what prompted him to do this, but it afforded me a great opportunity. First, I asked my students for another name for the square root symbol, which is called the *rad*ical sign. What are the chances? I then placed a superscripted ^{2} for squared at end of the symbol along with = Raad, resulting in $\sqrt{\text{Raad}}^{\,2}$ = Raad. This served as a perfect lead into discussing inverse operations (operations that undo one another, such as adding and subtracting, multiplying and dividing, and of course squaring and taking the square root).

When I retired at the end of the year, the students presented me with a class picture that they all had signed. Raad signed it as follows: $\sqrt{\text{Raad}}^{\,2}$. I'll never forget it!

VII

DEVELOPING STUDENT PARTICIPATION

52. Don't Let Them off the Hook

For various reasons, students will sometimes say, "I don't know" when asked a question. Don't let them off the hook. Do everything you can to elicit a response. Oftentimes, proximity works well. Get close to the student and lower your voice. Make statements such as, "You can do this, Karen." If this proves fruitless, ask simpler background questions just to get them started or provide prompts. Then work your way toward the original question. Be sure to give the student some positive feedback once an answer is offered. This helps to inspire confidence, which often leads to increased participation on the part of the student.

53. Humour Can Increase Participation and Attentiveness

I used to tell my students, "Don't be afraid to make a mistake. You know, I made a mistake once." This would draw a few chuckles as I paused briefly and then said," No really, I did, ... so I got married again!" Needless to say, they usually laughed hysterically. Then, I would say, "You see, we all make mistakes and I hope this is something that will never happen to you."

By showing your humanity and using humour, you can reach a lot of your students. The net result will be increased attentiveness and participation.

54. Choice Empowers Students

Let's assume that you will soon be starting a new geography unit. Perhaps you will be studying two of our nation's many natural resource industries such as mining, petroleum, forestry, agriculture, or fishing. Have a brief discussion with your class; then ask students to choose the industries they find most interesting. Caution: Give yourself enough lead time to properly prepare for the chosen unit of study.

If you are planning a field trip to the theatre, let your students choose which of the upcoming productions they would like to attend. Have them conduct a simple cost-benefit analysis to determine which is the better choice, especially if the two shows are at different venues or in different cities.

55. Two Claps Gets Everyone Involved

You never know when you'll find a great idea to use in your classroom. I picked up this one from a basketball clinic after I'd been teaching for over 30 years and modified it somewhat to suit my needs. Here's how it works using Johnny as an example:

1. When Johnny gives a really good answer, the teacher says, "Two claps for Johnny."
2. Led by the teacher, the whole class claps twice and together we say his name out loud.
3. At first, some students might be hesitant to participate. Tell them that you'll keep doing this until everyone gets involved and they are all "in sync." It may take a few tries, but eventually they'll all join in.

Two claps is a very effective tool for students such as Johnny. It builds confidence that they can provide praiseworthy answers that are appreciated by their teachers and peers at a level beyond a simple "good answer" response.

My students really enjoyed this activity and it kept the class alive and focused.

Sometimes, I would get a good answer and start to move on, only to hear, "Two claps, sir?" When I retired, some of my students presented me with a giant card signed by many of my current and former students. Several students had signed it "Two claps for Mr. Gomes." For me, this was a Hallmark moment.

56. Get Instant Feedback with a Show of Hands

Ask students frequently for a show of hands to encourage student engagement. For example, you could ask them: How many had breakfast today? Who is going to the football game Friday night? How many had difficulty with last night's homework? Just a couple of these survey-type questions and you've got virtually the whole class participating right from the get-go. This simple technique often allows you to start a discussion where you can ask more thought-provoking questions. Sometimes such instant feedback can change the direction of your lesson, e.g., extra review may be needed before moving on.

57. Lay Down a Challenge

If you're looking for a natural motivator, laying down a challenge is hard to beat. Students love a challenge and a chance to prove their teacher wrong by surpassing expectations. Just follow these three easy steps:

+ Place a challenge problem on the board at the start of the period or right after the completion of a lesson, e.g., "Today's Challenge" or "Problem of the Week."
+ Tell your students you think that fewer than 30% of them will get the correct solution, and that they should prove you wrong.
+ Set a time limit and watch them dig in.

Don't set the bar (estimated percentage) too low, but give them a fighting chance. If they beat your estimate, tell them you're impressed with both their tenacity and their skill. Give them two claps or maybe even three (see Tip 55).

58. Words of the Day

Although certain words may be known to all of your students, oftentimes their meanings are not fully understood. My personal favourite is the word recreation. Ask for its meaning and a common response is "to play," or "to enjoy a leisure activity." Its deeper meaning is most probably lost due to its pronunciation as *rec·re·a·tion*. If we examine its prefix and root word, we get *re·creation*, which means to restore or refresh one's spirit. Run this one by your peers and you'll be surprised how many of them miss the deeper meaning of "recreation."

During the course of a lesson, use a word or two many will not recognize or know the meaning of, e.g., "kudos," or "myriad." Post them on the board under Words of the Day and ask for the meaning. These words can then be used as the basis for a word wall. This cross-curricular activity is a fun way to develop student vocabulary, and it gives students who may be weaker in math and science a chance to shine.

59. Promote Your Subject Area

Many secondary school teachers and some teachers at the elementary level teach one or two subjects only, usually in their areas of expertise. Having a natural affinity for what they do makes the job of promoting their subject area an enjoyable task. I have a great deal of respect and admiration for teachers at the elementary level who teach many subjects across the curriculum and embrace each as if it were their specialty.

Here are a few promotional suggestions across a variety of subject areas:

◆ Travel with your students whenever possible. They are naturally attracted to courses in which travel is a key component. Take your students to a historical museum, science centre, or theatre. Have them make photo collages based on their trip. Post these pictures in your classroom and display cases around the school.

◆ Have students write a report on a topic in the news, the best of which will appear in each publication of your school newspaper and/or be posted on your website—for example, in science, a report on honey bees disappearing across North America or Asian carp setting to invade the Great Lakes.

- In a geography or travel and tourism class, create a contest to develop a brochure for a certain destination. Make contact with a local travel agency. They may provide helpful suggestions or even serve as judges for the contest. Develop local tourism by making your town or region the destination. Work with your local tourist bureau in this regard.

Many of these ideas present cross-curricular opportunities. Arrange with a colleague for English students from higher grades to serve as editors of your students' work. Such cross-grade groupings can be highly effective and benefit students at both grade levels.

Make use of local media as much as possible. Get the message out that your students are doing great things.

60. Have Contingency Plans for Unprepared Students

Unfortunately, there are days when students aren't prepared, and it just may be their group's day to make a presentation to the class. A little pre-planning can help reduce the number of these instances a great deal. Any big project should require a series of checks along the way (topic and objectives, sources consulted and first draft, to mention a few). Even with checks in place, there may still be problems due to illness and other unforeseen circumstances. Always have a Plan B in your back pocket. Be ready to continue on with another lesson or activity, if necessary.

61. Specialty Bulletin Boards

It's absolutely amazing how much talent and initiative there is in a single school. For example, two sisters at my school collected hundreds of old soccer jerseys to ship to needy children in Africa. Other students distinguished themselves in other ways—one by winning a national drama competition and another by breaking the world record in the 50 m breaststroke. Incredible! Every school has its stars, and whether they are current or former students of your school, they are role models for those who follow.

Have students design a bulletin board to showcase your school's "Students in the News," and name the board after your school mascot, e.g., "Sabres In The News." Local papers are usually loaded with stories about activities involving students from area schools. Larger daily newspapers are another good source. Don't limit these articles to school activities only—include any newsworthy, positive activity regarding your school's students.

> **Hint:** Create a specialty bulletin board for your subject area, such as Math In The News.

62. Develop a Buddy System for Backup

On one of your Day One handouts, create a spot for students to include contact information for at least two classmates or buddies who will provide them with backup in the event of an absence. Allow students to move about the room for no more than 90 seconds to obtain this information and return to their seats.

Buddy responsibilities should include:

- passing on homework information to an absent buddy;
- collecting extra handouts and getting these to their friend;
- photocopying or lending notes;
- keeping the buddy apprised of upcoming tests or assignments; and
- informing the teacher when the absent buddy is likely to return.

The buddy system affords absent students an opportunity to stay up to date and mitigates the effects of their absences. At the same time, it reduces the burden on the teacher both while the students are away and upon their return.

63. Small Group Activities

Small group activities allow us to teach and learn from one another. The greatest strength behind such collaborative learning is that we each bring our own unique experiences and varied skill sets to the table. In a group, we are often exposed to ideas and strategies we may not have considered on our own. A well-designed collaborative activity should be a benefit to all in the group. At the same time, such activities afford teachers the opportunity to observe student interactions and help out where needed.

Take time to design your groups and have at least one strong student in each. Let students know that every person has individual strengths. This point was made clear to me during my first year of teaching. I was using a projector—a one-of-a-kind in my school. Of course, it broke down, and hard as I tried, I just couldn't fix it. Ryan, who was one of my weakest students at the time, jumped up and offered his help. To my surprise, he had it fixed it no time. Lessons learned: first, we can all learn from one another, and second, don't get caught by equipment failure. Know how to operate classroom technology, including software.

64. Peer Tutors: A Win, Win, Win Scenario

When many students need help at once, a teacher can be spread too thin. To better meet the needs of your students, the development of a peer tutoring system for after school or lunchtime help is a winning enterprise.

Win #1: Students get the help they need.
Win #2: Tutors accrue volunteer hours.
Win #3: The teacher is freed up to float and assist where needed.

Begin the process by encouraging all students who want to improve their grades to attend—even A students may want to try to achieve an A+. Ask your A students to volunteer as tutors. You may have to approach shy students individually to get them involved in either capacity. Obtaining the support of parents is often vital to the success of such a program. Inform parents of these opportunities. Send a check box-style letter home requiring a parental signature that presents options such as:

- your child is progressing well, but is still welcome to come for tutoring;
- your child should come after school for extra help on specified days and times; or

- your child is off to an excellent start and should consider becoming a volunteer tutor.

It may take some legwork to get this up and running, but for me it was more than worthwhile as it proved to be a highly effective and very popular program. On occasion, I had more than half the students I taught involved and I had to use two classrooms to accommodate the more than 40 students in attendance.

Hints:

- Give each tutor only one or two students to help.
- Have the tutor sit in the middle if assisting two students.
- If you are having trouble getting enough peer tutors, ask students from higher grades.

65. Each Student Is Valuable

The importance of treating each student with respect cannot be overstated. This alone will speak to the fact they are valued. Don't get me wrong, I've had my share of challenging students over the years, but I've always tried to get through to them. When I did, they became some of the most rewarding students to teach.

We've all seen the student who is a thorn in almost every teacher's side. Yet, he or she seems to get along fine with a particular teacher. Perhaps the student just happens to like that teacher's subject a great deal. However, it's more likely that the teacher has not only treated the student respectfully, but has found a way to connect via one of his or her outside interests (see Tip 8).

You can bolster student confidence by offering sincere positive feedback (see Tip 68). Often we have no idea of the emotional baggage that our students may be carrying around. A simple kind word or acknowledgement for something well done may mean the world to them. Early in my career, I saw one of our senior teachers stop a student in the hall. I overheard him say, "Julie, it's a real pleasure to have you in my class." It's something I have never forgotten, and I doubt that Julie has either.

VIII

MOTIVATING STUDENTS AND YOURSELF

66. Vary Your Approach

Use a variety of teaching techniques and activities to maintain student interest; after all, variety is the spice of life. Avoid the trap of failing to change classroom routines, such as starting every class with bell work. If you like to use bell work frequently, vary the activities from day to day. Many math teachers like to start off classes by taking up homework on the board. You can shake things up by using homework pairs instead (see Tip 45). Provide lessons that address all three learning styles—visual, auditory, and kinesthetic. Small group activities involving the use of manipulatives, such as math cards, fit the bill. Break a 70-minute period into several different activities—it won't take long for you to gauge the effective time span for an activity with a particular class. This will help avoid monotony and will result in increased student focus and participation.

67. Setting and Raising the Bar

Set the bar high and maintain your standards. Students need to be challenged. Anyone can improve math skills or their ability to speak a new language with a little practice. Even problem-solving skills can be enhanced through practice and by exploring different approaches to this type of problem. If you engage students, they will be motivated and rise to your level of expectation. As the course progresses and your students have become familiar with you, raise the bar even higher. "Always keep improving" should be a mantra for both students and teachers.

68. Positive Feedback

Supplying positive feedback is an essential component of successful teaching. This form of praise, however, must be deserved and not falsely given. Balance this with a healthy dose of constructive criticism, as students need to be made aware of areas for improvement. Some positive feedback strategies are listed below:

- Use Two Claps (see Tip 55) for especially good answers or the first time a shy student answers voluntarily.
- Give verbal praise. A good answer by a student affords an opportunity for positive feedback, e.g., "That's right, Carla," or "Well done, Eric."
- Use written comments when checking homework or marking papers, e.g., "Strong effort," or "Terrific work, Shauna."
- Make a "Wow List" (see Tip 98) when grading papers.
- Encourage students to applaud after a student makes a presentation to the class.
- Take advantage of one-on-one opportunities, such as passing in the hallway. This is a great time to give positive feedback that isn't phony. For example: "George, it's a real pleasure to be your teacher—you add a great deal to our class." Or, "Amanda, I was really impressed with the contributions you made to your group today. Keep up the good work." Or, "Gary, you did a much better job on your homework. That's the kind of effort I'm looking for."

According to Rev. Robert H. Schuller, "It takes but one positive thought when given a chance to survive and thrive to overpower an entire army of negative thoughts." By supplying positive feedback, we can plant seeds and watch them grow.

69. Keep It Real

Real-life examples, especially if local in nature, are interest magnets. Students just love to talk about their favourite pizza place, new retail stores, or an upcoming local festival. Be on the lookout for any real-life advertisement, product, or situation that helps illustrate a point or concept. Here are a few examples:

- Newspaper ads and flyers are great for consumer education, mathematics, and critical thinking. One of my all-time favourites was an ad that said your dollar is worth $1.50. Well, initially, many of us would think that this represented a 50% savings. Let's take a closer look. It follows that your $100 would be worth $150. Thus, you would pay $100 for any item in the store that usually sells for $150. Your savings then is actually $50 on a $150 item. This represents a savings of one-third, about 33%, not 50%. Although this ad got patrons in the door, I'm sure it caused more than a few problems at the cash register.
- Packaging is wonderful for studying 3D shapes, e.g., Toblerone triangular prisms.
- A recent accident involving alcohol may be worth discussing or studying prior to prom night.

Guest speakers on a variety of topics are often available free of charge. Many businesses and government agencies supply this educational service as part of their public relations and community service programs. Provide school administration with the individual's name and business or agency well in advance. In order to avoid surprises and possible embarrassing situations, do some vetting of the speaker. Provide guidelines and find out the details and content of the speaker's presentation early on.

Invite a local author into your classroom. You may be surprised to find out how many there are in your own community. Students at all levels can learn a great deal from these experts. Be sure to prep your students in advance and let them create and submit a list of questions that they would like to ask the speaker. Have a backup plan in case your speaker has to cancel unexpectedly, is late, or finishes earlier than expected.

70. Music Is a Powerful Classroom Tool

Music is a powerful tool that is readily accessible. YouTube videos are available for almost any song. Lessons have been enriched by such classics as Gordon Lightfoot's "Canadian Railroad Trilogy," Bob Dylan's "With God On Our Side," or Harry Chapin's "Cat's In The Cradle." Use of current tunes is especially motivating, but be sure to check out the lyrics for appropriate content first.

Amy Burvall, a teacher at Le Jardin Academy in Kailua, Hawaii (International Baccalaureate Middle Years Program) has taken the use of music in the classroom to a whole new level by creating her own videos, which are pop music satires soaked with history and literature lessons (www.amyburvall.wix.com/ edupunk). Co-creator of the *History for Music Lovers* YouTube channel, Amy performs in costume in many of the videos, e.g., "The French Revolution" to the tune of Lady Gaga's "Bad Romance" and "Elizabeth I" to "She's Not There," a sixties song by the Zombies. (See Tip 48 on video clips.)

71. Competition Gets the Adrenalin Flowing

Coaches regularly use competition to improve players' performance. Effective drills pit team members against the clock or each other. This tool can be used in the classroom as well. You may start off with some bell work on times tables to see how many correct answers a student achieves in one minute. Provide enough questions so that your best students will be challenged. Let them soar. Repeating this activity should result in increased proficiency and improved scores. My students would always get revved up for these timed events.

Hints:

- Provide 30 questions, divided into three equal groups. Only the two best groups of 10 will count, resulting in a mark out of 20. A student who gets 29 correct answers still gets 20 out of 20. This can encourage students to push themselves.
- Give students a dry run or two before counting the results. This helps students establish a comfort level for dealing with time constraints.

There are numerous math and science contests and competitions at both the elementary and secondary school levels. Creative writing and speech competitions abound and robotics competitions have taken off in recent years. Consider starting or lending a hand to an existing club to help students prepare for competition. Not only does this help students to improve their performance, but any awards also add to their resumes and may make a difference when they apply for university and college programs, bursaries, and scholarships.

72. Celebration Lifts Everyone's Spirits

Take advantage of opportunities to celebrate with your students. Rejoice in their accomplishments in all areas, not just academics. You can celebrate:

- very good verbal answers with Two Claps (see Tip 55);
- excellent test answers by making a Wow List (see Tip 98);
- improved performance—print certificates such as "Star of the Week" and "Student of the Month" to honour students who show the most improvement, and award each honouree with a certificate to take home and post a copy in your classroom;
- special accomplishments by posting them on your bulletin board (see Tip 61);
- improved behaviour by acknowledging students with positive comments (see Tip 68); and
- special events such as birthdays, holidays, and school-wide celebrations by recognizing them in creative and appropriate ways.

Celebrating student success should not be reserved only for those obtaining A grades. More importantly, look for ways to celebrate improvement, as student success should be measured from individual starting points. Academically, look for progress in the class median, the distribution of letter grades across the class, and the grades of individuals. Socially, look to recognize improvements in the affective domain, such as being on time, listening skills, increased participation, social interaction within groups, homework completion, and other responsible behaviours.

73. Travel: An Experience Like No Other

In recent years, I have climbed Gros Morne in western Newfoundland, stood atop Half Dome in California's Yosemite National Park, and hiked through the Valley of the Ten Peaks up to Sentinel Pass in Banff National Park, Alberta. When it comes to travel, you can read about it, listen to others talk about it, or even watch a film about it, but nothing takes the place of experiencing it for yourself.

Travel opportunities offer students unique experiences. They allow both teacher and student to see the world and each other in a different light. Travelling with students is not without risk, but usually the rewards far outweigh the problems. I once took 40 students out west to British Columbia for eight days. When the plane took off, some of them began to cheer, much to the surprise of the other passengers and myself. I didn't realize many of the students had never flown before. That was a "wow" moment for me.

Before travelling with your students, carefully review school board field trip policies and procedures. Follow the intent of these regulations and take a copy along to ensure that you remember required protocols in case of an emergency.

Whether it's with a team, a club, or your class, travel with students when you get the chance. You'll probably come away tired, if not exhausted, but more importantly, you'll be enriched and motivated by the experience.

74. Inspirational Quotations for Students and Teachers

Top Ten for Students

It is a constant challenge to keep students motivated. Here is a list of my top ten quotations to inspire students to perform at a high level:

1. "There is no elevator to success, you have to take the stairs." (Anonymous)
2. "Believe you can and you're halfway there." (Theodore Roosevelt)
3. "By failing to prepare, you are preparing to fail." (Benjamin Franklin)
4. "The difference between ordinary and extraordinary is that little extra." (Anonymous)
5. "In the beginning, you make your habits. In the end, your habits make you." (Anonymous)
6. "Your future is created by what you do today, not tomorrow." (Robert Kiyosaki)
7. "Success is not final, failure is not fatal. It is the courage to continue that counts." (Winston Churchill)
8. "Plan your work for today and every day, then work your plan." (Margaret Thatcher)
9. "If you don't have time to do it right, when will you have time to do it over?" (John Wooden)
10. "Good, better, best. Never let it rest, until your good is better and your better best." (Anonymous)

Top Ten for Teachers

Don't forget to keep yourself motivated. No matter how upbeat you are, from time to time you'll need a boost. These quotations should do the trick:

1. "In a completely rational society, the best of us would be teachers and the rest of us would have to settle for something else." (Lee Iacocca)
2. "If your plan is for a year, plant rice. If your plan is for a decade, plant trees. If your plan is for a lifetime, educate children." (Confucius)
3. "A teacher affects eternity; he can never tell where his influence stops." (Henry Adams)
4. "What a teacher writes on the blackboard of life can never be erased." (Anonymous)
5. "Better than a thousand days of diligent study is one day with a great teacher." (Japanese proverb)
6. "What nobler employment, or more valuable to the state, than that of the man who instructs the rising generation." (Marcus Tullius Cicero)
7. "If kids come to us from strong, healthy, functioning families, it makes our jobs easier. If they do not come to us from strong, healthy, functioning families, it makes our job more important." (Barbara Coloroso)
8. "Those who can, do. Those who can do more, teach." (Anonymous)
9. "Technology is just a tool. In terms of getting the kids working together and motivating them, the teacher is the most important." (Bill Gates)
10. "You can't let praise or criticism get to you. It's a weakness to get caught up in either one." (John Wooden)

Post your favourite inspirational quotation where you will see it daily. I keep mine, the words of Eric Butterworth, in my study at home. I'm happy to share it with you here.

"Don't *go* through life; *grow* through life."

Each time I see it, I am reminded of how I want to live.

75. Ten Inspirational Films for Teachers

Make time to watch these inspirational movies and let your spirit soar!

1. *Goodbye, Mr. Chips* (1939)
2. *To Sir, with Love* (1967)
3. *Up the Down Staircase* (1967)
4. *Stand and Deliver* (1988)
5. *Dead Poets Society* (1989)
6. *Lean on Me* (1989)
7. *Mr. Holland's Opus* (1995)
8. *Coach Carter* (2005)
9. *Freedom Writers* (2007)
10. *Beyond the Blackboard* (2011)

A common theme throughout these movies is that teachers face many challenges. Yes, even outstanding teachers experience setbacks, but they do not give up. They bounce back and continually strive to reach all of their students, even under the most difficult of circumstances.

76. Play the Cards You've Been Dealt

The greatest satisfactions in teaching don't come from the straight-A students who achieve a final mark of 95% in your class, but from those who show the most improvement and personal growth.

I remember starting my first year of teaching. Fresh out of teacher's college, briefcase in hand, I was ready to change the world. After grading my first Grade 10 geography mapping assignment on the continents of the world, I was shocked and discouraged by some of the results. One student titled his work, "Map of the Contents." Another labelled his continents with no "r" or "i" in many of the words such as "Afica" and North and South "Ameca." This was a reality check for me. I truly never envisioned such poor work from high school students. My point is, rather than becoming discouraged, learn to expect anything and play the cards you've been dealt. Be proactive. Recognize that some of these difficulties stem from learning disabilities that have gone undetected. Seek the assistance of relevant support staff. The more challenges students face, the more they will need your help, and the more room there is for improvement.

77. Maintain an Even Keel

Finding a balance between work, family, and taking care of my health was one of my greatest challenges throughout my teaching career. Though many different winds will blow, try to maintain an even keel by adopting some of these suggestions:

◆ Be wary of over-committing yourself.

- Watch something that makes you laugh.
- Converse with your best friend; arrange to meet for coffee, if possible.
- Make time for yourself. Get regular exercise to reduce anxiety and stress levels.
- Read a good book about one of your interests or hobbies.
- Join a yoga class and roll the benefits of exercise and meditation into one. A colleague recently told me that joining yoga was a life-altering experience for her as it has been for me.
- Take a vacation to get away from it all.

The words of a trusted friend ring true: "You've got to build regular personal time into your schedule." Do this and you will come away refreshed and motivated to perform at a high level.

78. When Things Go Wrong

Things don't always go as planned. If your lesson flopped, take time to evaluate what went wrong. Here are some things to consider. When did things start to fall apart? Did you put adequate time into preparing your lesson? Did you start promptly? Were students engaged from the beginning? Was the lesson well paced? Did you make your expectations and instructions clear to your students? Were your activities so difficult that students lost interest? Did you provide time guidelines for completion of activities?

A lesson that falls apart can be extremely discouraging and it can challenge a teacher's confidence. Though you are bound to be upset, the sooner you begin to self-evaluate and look at this as a growth opportunity, the better off you'll be.

Don't throw the lesson out just because you've had a problem. It may only need tweaking. In fact, the lesson may not be the problem at all. It may have fallen apart because of your inability to handle an unforeseen problem with a student. This may be the perfect time to call on your colleagues (see Tip 35).

Teachers should always be involved in self-evaluation. Reinvigorate yourself; find solutions by evaluating your lesson planning and delivery. Even great lessons can be improved upon.

79. Have Fun Every Day

At the start of a new school year or semester, I loved to play the "roller board gag" on my Grade 9s. The roller board was a flexible "blackboard" with three panels that looped around two large rollers. The rollers were positioned at the top and bottom and were hidden from view by aluminum mouldings, the top one adjacent to the ceiling. Each panel could be viewed individually by sliding the board up or down. Prior to the start of class, I would write science notes such as chemistry formulas or Bohr diagrams on one or two of the panels, then roll them up to hide these notes. On the third panel, I would write information pertinent to my class and leave it there for all to see.

Once I had discussed this information, I would roll down the next panel, which was covered with science notes. Due to the roller board's design, it appeared to descend from the ceiling. I would say, "It looks like Mr. B. is using the board upstairs again. We'll just have to check back later." Then I would continue my lesson without skipping a beat, leaving many of the students bewildered. Some of them would be half bent over in their seats trying to solve the mystery, to no avail. Watching them contort themselves made it tough not to spill the beans right away. Later, I would roll the board down a little further, exposing more of the science notes. "Darn it," I'd say. "It looks like he's still using our board." Eventually, I'd come clean and we'd have a good laugh at no one's expense in particular. My students got a big kick out of this prank and they learned something about critical thinking. Having a little fun every day will help keep both you and your students motivated.

80. Mentoring New Teachers

New teachers face many challenges. Even if things appear to be okay on the surface, don't assume all is well. Take time to ask them how their classes are going. Listen carefully to their concerns. Provide constructive suggestions and offer your help if needed. Making new teachers feel welcome and providing some support will boost their spirits, and let them know that they are not alone in the struggles they face.

Many school boards offer mentoring programs for new teachers. If you can spare the time, volunteer to become a teacher mentor. This can be a very rewarding and rejuvenating experience.

81. Get Outside Your Comfort Zone

One day, early in my career, I was walking by the music room when I was asked to join the teachers' skit on "The Twelve Days of Christmas." I wondered, "How bad can it be? There'll be at least 11 other teachers on stage." So I decided to join in and soon found out I'd be personifying "seven swans a-swimming." Someone handed me a white tutu—complete with a giant bow for my hair and a pair of white leotards. I wasn't surprised to find out that the English teacher who had volunteered for the part had bolted the scene when he saw his costume. Apparently, I was it—all six foot four and 170 pounds of me. To say that I was nervous was an understatement—petrified was more like it. I knew the show must go on, so I decided to take one for the team.

It was agonizing waiting backstage at the packed Christmas assembly as they worked their way up to seven swans a-swimming. Finally, I made my entrance, totally unrehearsed. I began tippy toeing across the stage with my fingertips atop my head and my lengthy arms raised to form the shape of a heart. The crowd went absolutely wild! Talk about raising the roof. Next, I broke into the breaststroke before taking my place in line. I couldn't get off the stage yet as we had to get through to "twelve drummers drumming." After what seemed like an eternity, we began to exit the stage and for whatever reason, on came the music to "Suzie Snowflake." The next thing I knew, one of the other teachers grabbed me and began doing a waltz, and of course he was much shorter than I. There was nowhere to hide so I persevered, and in the end it was great fun.

I've had many students tell me it's something they'll never forget. My participation in this crazy event demonstrated to students a willingness to have fun and share a laugh as part of a team. It built a bridge that would be hard to duplicate in a classroom setting.

IX

COMMUNICATING WITH PARENTS IS ESSENTIAL

82. Send Policies Home for Parental Signatures

At the beginning of a term or semester, send your classroom policies and important information home for parents to read, sign, and return the next day. Ask your students to encourage their parents to read these policies carefully before signing them. Supply parents with the following information:

- a course outline;
- an evaluation policy (see Tip 21);
- your policy for missed tests and late assignments (see Tip 21);
- student responsibilities, such as making every effort to be on time daily (see Tip 16), homework completion (see Tip 20), and being present on test days (see Tips 21 and 90);
- teacher availability for extra help—include days and times (see Tip 24);
- favourite websites that offer additional help in your subject area; and
- teacher availability for parental contact, and best times to be reached along with phone number and extension (see Tip 24).

Having your policies and important information in place and in the hands of parents early on will save you problems down the road.

Hint: Be proactive. Share your classroom policies with school administration prior to sending them home.

Such courtesies are appreciated by administrators and may help to ward off unforeseen problems.

83. Connecting with Parents

As soon as you realize that a student is functioning below grade level, get in touch with a parent. Make your calls around the dinner hour or on a weekend morning. Most parents will be glad to hear from you and thank you for your concern.

Have a plan in mind to achieve student success and work with the parent to make it happen. Some students may be unable to attend after-school extra help sessions due to transportation difficulties or babysitting responsibilities. In such cases, try to find a volunteer peer tutor to go to their home—perhaps a current or former student. To help make the process of developing an action plan run smoothly:

- identify problem areas prior to calling the parent;
- note the date and name of the parent you speak with;
- record any pertinent insights offered by the parent;
- develop an action plan with the parent;
- inform the parent of upcoming evaluations; and
- give a timeframe for contacting the parent again to discuss the student's progress.

Some teachers prefer to keep in contact with parents via e-mail. This is a personal choice. Using e-mail avoids wasting time playing phone tag and allows for more frequent communication. Drawbacks regarding e-mail are that it often leads to miscommunication and can make teachers vulnerable to overly zealous parents who demand daily or weekly contact that is time consuming and often unnecessary. Regardless, connecting with parents and having them actively involved in the action plan is an important component for student success.

84. Keeping Grades and Parents Current

With the advent of computer programs, keeping student marks up to date is relatively easy. After each major test, provide a year-to-date grade or cumulative percent right on the test and ask each student to take it home for signing. This works extremely well. For parents, it's like getting a report card after every major test, which often prompts them to call the teacher and cuts down on playing phone tag. Consider including a section on the test for both a parental comment and signature. Use a simple checklist to keep a record of parental signatures. Ensure that students return signed tests by assigning firm penalties for those who don't.

85. Teacher Websites Keep Everyone Informed

A teacher's website can be a valuable tool for parent and student alike. For things to run smoothly, the teacher should update the website regularly, if not daily. Suggested items to include in your website are:

- a course calendar showing test and assignment dates;
- course information sheets and course outline;
- various policies, procedures and classroom rules;
- daily homework;
- links to course-specific resources;
- extra help schedule;
- updated marks; and
- a blog about what's going on in the classroom.

Do you need help to learn how to make a website or a blog? Try Google Sites, weebly.com, or wordpress.com. Many schools have a teacher designated to assist colleagues with technology concerns.

86. Have a Student Secretary for Parent-Teacher Interviews

Select a volunteer from one of your classes to act as your secretary during parent-teacher interviews. Thank the student for volunteering. Familiarize the student with both the benefits and the secretary's role as outlined below.

Benefits:

- The student secretary accumulates valuable volunteer hours.
- The student also gains experience dealing with adults.
- This illustrates to parents that teachers see their students as valuable by empowering them and by providing growth opportunities.
- It sets a professional tone for the meeting.
- It helps the parent-teacher interview process run much more smoothly.
- It saves the teacher time.

The Secretary's Role:

- Greet parents in a friendly manner.
- Set up appointment times if not prearranged.
- Distribute a welcome sheet (see Tip 87).
- Take down contact information of parents who arrived but were unable to stay.

- Keep the teacher on schedule.

There may be no better time to make a good impression on parents than on this night. Having a student secretary can help you make the most of it.

87. Provide a Welcome Sheet for Parent-Teacher Interviews

After welcoming parents, the student secretary should supply them with a welcome sheet that may contain:

- a warm, inviting title such as Welcome to Parent-Teacher Interviews;
- your name, subject, meeting room number, and interview time;
- an introductory paragraph that thanks parents for attending and lets them know you are looking forward to the opportunity of discussing their child's progress with them;
- contact information such as phone number and extension (and/or professional e-mail address at your discretion), and times when you can be reached;
- times when extra help is available for any student who seeks to improve;
- information regarding tutoring programs that are available at your school—high achievers may wish to become peer tutors (see Tip 64);
- a MEMO section that provides information about policies or procedures you wish to highlight (e.g., frequency of major tests, the need for parental signatures and the meaning of the year-to-date mark), upcoming tests and

assignments, and what students are currently studying; and

- a NOTES section where parents can write important information discussed during the interview.

A well-designed and informative welcome sheet demonstrates that you are organized, well prepared, and thoughtful. It also helps to set the tone for a professional encounter. As an added benefit, the welcome sheet is a huge time saver, cutting the length of many interviews in half.

88. What Parents Really Want to Know

This list is based on my personal experience of teaching full-time for 35 years and conducting in excess of 1,500 parent-teacher interviews. Parents want to know:

- current grade and most recent results;
- behaviour—positive or negative;
- homework completion;
- participation, including how students relate to their peers;
- areas for improvement, both academic and behavioural;
- upcoming evaluations; and
- action plan to improve student grades and resolve other issues.

Being able to address each of the above items accurately will require some record keeping in the form of checklists and anecdotal comments.

> **Hint:** Don't be surprised that the majority of parents who show up for interviews are the parents of high achievers. Therefore, it is a good idea to either send a note home

or call the parents you need to see the most to set up an interview.

89. How to Shine When Conducting a Parent-Teacher Interview

Smile and thank parents for coming in. Begin by accentuating the positive, touching on any of the items from What Parents Really Want to Know (see Tip 88). Next, bring to light any areas for improvement of the student in question, e.g., incomplete homework, lack of participation, and behaviour issues. This provides a framework for developing an action plan. Then, ask parents for their concerns and keep an open mind, even if they are critical. Once again, accentuate the positive then formulate an action plan along with the parents; their involvement in the process is often fundamental to your success.

Having made at least one previous phone contact with parents is extremely helpful when conducting a formal parent-teacher interview. You can still follow the outline above if an action plan already exists. You will need to provide updates and modify the action plan if necessary. It is paramount that parents realize that your primary goal is student success.

During the interview, listen carefully, and make pertinent notes. Obtain any contact information you may require. Let parents know how and when you will be in touch with them. For example, tell them when the next important evaluation will be sent home for signing and when they can expect either a note or a phone call to update them on their child's progress. Follow through on your part of the plan and if the student fails to cooperate fully, contact the parents immediately. If the time allotted for the interview turns out to be insufficient, make arrangements to contact the parents the next day to complete your discussion.

X

EFFECTIVE TESTING PRACTICES

90. Posting Test Dates

Try to give at least one week's notice for any major test. Obtain student input when choosing the date. You will make life difficult for yourself if you insist on testing on a day when some of your students will be away at a sporting event or gone on a field trip. Be aware of special timetables or planned fire alarm practices that may interrupt your test or reduce its allotted time. The sooner you decide on a date the better chance students will have to rework appointments. Make it understood that you expect every student to be present on test dates. You may decide to adopt the same attendance policy for your test days as for school exam days.

91. Cheating Is Serious

A few days before the first test, have a serious talk about academic integrity, including:

- ◆ the purpose of the test, which is to find out what the student knows, not what someone else knows;
- ◆ exactly what materials students will be allowed to have on their desk, e.g., any required supplies must be taken out prior to the test and pencil cases must be kept under their seats;
- ◆ each student's responsibility to sit up straight, and keep answer sheets squarely in front of them and covered if possible;
- ◆ not letting their eyes wander;
- ◆ never bringing cheat sheets of any type including writing on hands or arms; and

- the fact that a student's grade will never recover from getting a zero on a major test because of cheating.

    Hint: If a student is eyeing you during a test, it may mean that he or she is about to cheat. Immediately walk by the student's desk to deter this from happening. Our goal here is to help the student avoid doing something foolish.

Before every test I remind students, as they used to say in the McDonalds' commercial, to "Keep your eyes on your fries." It may not mean exactly what I'm trying to convey, but they get my drift. Students really eat this stuff up, if you'll pardon the pun. They love hearing lines from commercials and songs. So give it a try—who cares if they think you're "hip" or a "dip?" It still gets their attention.

92. Test Review Is Only Fair

Good teachers practice various forms of ongoing review. The use of formative assessment tools (quizzes, checklist, and anecdotal comments) gives both teacher and student valuable feedback with respect to student learning. Ongoing review can be embedded into daily lessons, which helps reduce student anxiety come test time and allows the teacher to modify instruction as needed.

If you have access to a student response system—which may include personal devices such as cell phones, tablets, or a class set of wireless clickers, this can be used for test review on an ongoing and/or summative basis. Such devices provide virtually instant feedback on true/false or multiple-choice questions allowing you to analyze individual student data and whole class data in real time. For example, you can determine the percentage of correct answers as well as which individuals were in error on any given question. Also, the class average and each student's total score are readily available. This information can then be used to identify which topics need more review and which students need additional tutoring.

If a comprehensive review is deemed necessary, it should cover the entire unit of study and not be limited to simple knowledge-type questions alone. Include a variety of question types such as applications and problem solving if such types are to be included on the test.

93. Don't Sacrifice Quality for Convenience

Be careful not to sacrifice quality for convenience by using too many easy-to-mark questions such as multiple-choice and fill-in-the-blank.

It is my belief that multiple-choice questions should be limited in number and scope. Students should be given the opportunity to illustrate what they know and gain part marks for their answers. Why should a student who knows little to nothing about a problem and a student who makes one error in an otherwise good solution both receive zero for their choice? This is a problem endemic to most multiple-choice tests. It can, however, be somewhat overcome by scoring each question out of three marks as follows:

3 marks for the correct answer
2 marks for choosing the second best answer
1 marks for the third best answer
0 for the worst answer

In my view, this technique is still fraught with problems. That said, colleges and universities still rely a great deal on multiple-choice testing. In order for our students to be prepared, try to include some multiple-choice questions on each major test.

Fill-in-the-blanks are one of my least favourite types of questions. They are often ambiguous and may have two or more reasonable or correct responses. Many teachers try to cover themselves by asking students to insert the best response. My feeling here is that a teacher should reward the student with any answer that makes sense. This illustrates the need for taking a great deal of care in the design of fill-in-the-blank-type questions. When I used this type of question, my instruction was to "Fill in the blanks with an appropriate response," allowing the flexibility to accept a range of reasonable answers.

94. Problem Solving

Tough problems are rarely solved promptly. In the words of Thomas Edison, "I've not failed. I've just found 10,000 ways that won't work." If we want students to be creative when problem solving, then we must allow some time for thinking, trial, and strategizing.

Consider giving students a choice regarding problem-solving questions. This seems to be done a great deal more on English and history tests, where students may be asked to write an essay on two of the three topics listed. Very seldom do we encounter such questions on math tests; I'm not sure why.

Give students the opportunity to show you what they know. Ask them to solve a problem in more than one way. Here the goals are measuring the breadth of students' knowledge and their ability to think creatively. Caution: This is a time-consuming question for both teacher and student. Tell students to make sure they complete all portions of the test first before trying to offer a second or third solution to this type of problem.

95. Write Your Answer Key in Advance

Writing your answer key in advance of photocopying helps avoid a multitude of mistakes. This often results in rewording questions to provide clarity or scaffolding a question to achieve a more comprehensive response. You are also more likely to catch errors than just by proofreading alone. When students ask lots of questions during a test, it's often the result of poor test design on the teacher's part. Writing your answers early will also help you judge the proper length and difficulty level of the test. Designing a fair test and allowing enough time for most, if not all, students to complete it are essential to effective evaluation.

> **Hint:** Hold back a page of the test until the next day if you feel it's too long.

96. Time Limits: Establish a Window

Encourage students to do their best. If they finish a test early, ask them to review their answers twice and leave no question blank. This involves reading the test questions carefully and reviewing their responses. At the same time, be a pragmatist and don't waste their time. For this reason, provide a minimum and maximum time limit for each test. Make students aware that once they turn their tests in, there is no getting them back.

For example, if the minimum time is 40 minutes, accept no test before this time. Review tests quickly at each student's desk and encourage them to try to complete blank responses. If you are satisfied with a student's effort, accept the test and provide the student with an activity to complete.

Keeping students engaged after the test discourages talking while other students are still working on test responses. This is a good time to reward your students with a relevant puzzle to solve or an interesting passage to read that relates to your next unit of study. At the maximum time, ask for all tests to be handed in, unless you feel you have misjudged the time required. A five-minute extension may be justified.

97. Limit Questions During a Test

Students should not ask the teacher questions during a test unless they believe they have discovered an error, an ambiguity, and/or awkward language. It could be a spelling error or an omission such as no marks allotted to a problem. If they have a point, write the correction on the board, then interrupt the class to make everyone aware of the correction or clarification. As hard as you may try, some errors, omissions, or ambiguities will occur from time to time on your tests or assignments.

Believe it or not, some students will ask you if their answer to a certain question is right! During a test, however, such content questions from students are strictly out of bounds.

98. Make a Wow List

Certain test answers just make the teacher say "Wow!" You will want to share these with the whole class. So, create a Wow List of excellent answers. If time permits, write the question numbers and the corresponding names on the board from your Wow List for students to see as they enter the room. Everyone loves seeing their name up on a marquee. It affords an opportunity to praise a weaker student who did well on a certain question or a stronger student who is shy about participating.

George was one of my weaker students and was shy about presenting in front of others. The first time he had a perfect solution on a math test his name went up on the board. For George, knowing that his answer was right took the stress out of having to present his solution to the class. Realizing that this was George's first presentation, I asked him to relax and take his time. With a little prompting, he did a marvellous job. I congratulated him for a job well done and the whole class followed up with two enthusiastic claps (see Tip 55).

99. Post Op: Evaluate and Adjust

Every test and assignment should be reevaluated once graded. The teacher should look for areas where students scored poorly. Then a decision has to be made on the validity of each question under scrutiny. Perhaps a question was poorly worded or beyond the expectations of the course. You may find it necessary to reduce the value of a question, e.g., mark it out of three instead of five, or drop it from the test or assignment entirely. If the question is deemed appropriate, then the teacher should be introspective. An excellent teacher will always ask, "What should I have done to improve student understanding of this concept?" and then adjust accordingly.

100. Dealing with Poor Results

If you are pleased with the class results on a test, be sure to let students know. Positive test results are, however, more about individuals. If some students are disappointed in their grades, they will find little comfort in the fact that most of their peers did well.

Prior to returning tests, inform students that some of them may be unhappy with their results. Request that they deal with their disappointment constructively, not by ripping up their test in anger. Once tests are returned, take a show of hands. Ask how many are not pleased with their grade; students these days tend to be up front about this. My question to them is, "What are you going to do about it?" You must give them hope and an action plan, and you'll want to be sure that parents are on board as well.

> **Hint:** Develop the action plan with the students. The more the ideas come from them, the more they'll be invested in the solution.

At this point, I usually relate a true story about my son David who was an A+ student in his high school calculus class. I'll never forget the time that he received only 47% on his midterm in a first-year university calculus course. Ouch! He was shocked, to say the least. Realizing that he must have missed an important concept, David developed his own action plan. He visited his high school calculus teacher who provided him with some resources to review, and soon sorted out his misunderstanding. He wrote out solutions to every question in his textbook related to his next university calculus test and as a result went on to achieve an almost perfect mark. Despite his first test score weighing him down, David earned a final grade of A– for the course. I couldn't have been more proud.

Not all disappointments come from failing grades. I often encountered students who had achieved very high math marks in Grade 8 but only average results on their first Grade 9 math test. To be sure, both they and their parents were disappointed. One such student was Melanie. It didn't take much convincing to get her in for extra help and we reviewed her problem areas. After getting help a few times her grades began to soar. Melanie earned an A+ final grade and became one of my peer tutors along the way. I'll never forget her sense of pride at what she had accomplished. Outstanding work, Melanie.

When almost the whole class does poorly on a certain assignment, test, or quiz, consider offering a "one-time special." First, tell the students why you have chosen to do this. Perhaps the quiz or assignment was too hard, your instructions weren't clear, or you hadn't fully prepared your students for it. Second, let them know that this is a one-time special that won't happen again. Third, spend time taking up the answers, paying particular attention to what they did well and what they did poorly. Finally, set a new date for your one-time special and let them know you're looking forward to seeing a great deal of improvement.

101. Taking Up Tests: Be Transparent

It is important that tests be taken up with your students for several reasons:

- Students need to be able to compare their answers to exemplary ones. This gives them a chance to make corrections and gain insights.
- Students are able to identify areas of weakness and find a focus for their action plans for improvement.
- It allows the teacher to justify the assigned grade.
- It reduces the number of questions to be remarked.

My students were keenly aware that I was approachable and that I wanted them to get the grades they deserved. This didn't mean that I lowered my standards in any way, but it often meant explaining a bit more about their errors or omissions, and if warranted, resulted in the raising of their grades.

Keep the whole evaluation process transparent. Students should have a clear understanding of the criteria used to evaluate each of their test questions. If you accomplish this, there will be little cause for concern.

LOOKING AHEAD

Surprise, wonder, discovery, enlightenment, and laughter—these are some of the joys that teachers and students hope to experience every day. But, inspiring events don't just happen with regularity when left to chance. To reap the rewards of teaching, you need to establish an effective learning environment that is structured and carefully planned—one that makes use of efficient routines and procedures; provides engaging lessons; fosters a caring, cooperative atmosphere; and motivates students to actively partake in the learning process. And this book can help you do exactly that.

I am delighted that you have chosen *Ready-Set-Teach!* as a part of your commitment to life-long learning. After 30-plus years as a teacher, this was an opportunity for me to give back to the educational community—to share something personal, with pride and passion. It is my hope and belief that this book will provide for you a framework for building a successful teaching career.

I've touched on topics that I know are most important to you as a teacher—connecting with your students right from the start, motivating students, modifying student behaviour, increasing student participation, and communicating effectively with parents. As you employ the practical strategies found within these pages your classroom will run more smoothly and efficiently, creating a learning environment you can be proud of—one your students will be happy to share.

Take a personal interest in every student in your room. Try not to let any of them fall through the cracks. Never forget that each pupil is valuable and must be treated with respect. Model for your students the positive behaviours that are so necessary for success in school and, more importantly, in life. The more creativity, energy, and enthusiasm you bring to your classroom, the more your students will enjoy themselves and learn.

As educators, we have the opportunity to touch lives—and affect them profoundly. Remember this and you'll stay motivated to "bring it" every day.

ABOUT THE AUTHOR

Jim Gomes graduated from the Faculty of Education at the University of Windsor and taught for over 35 years with the Greater Essex County District School Board in Southwestern Ontario. A master teacher of Grade 9 mathematics, Jim established a highly successful peer-tutoring program. Throughout his career, he also served as a mentor to new teachers. His influence and love of teaching reached beyond the classroom and into his own family. Inspired by their father, Jim's three children have all become teachers.

Beyond the classroom, Jim distinguished himself as a dedicated coach of over 50 school and community sports teams. He coached boys and girls from ages 5 to 18 in a variety of sports, including basketball, baseball, and volleyball.

In 2014, Jim founded J-Go LEARN Inc., an educational resource company with the express goal of maximizing teacher effectiveness and student learning. Jim is part of the Professional Learning Series at the Faculty of Education, University of Windsor, and he is available for seminars.

An avid traveller, Jim and his wife Pam enjoy hiking in wilderness areas of national parks in Canada and the United States.

To learn more about Jim Gomes and his creative pursuits, visit his website at:
www.JGoLearn.com

Jim welcomes your comments on this book.
You can reach him via e-mail at:
jim@jgolearn.com

NOTES

NOTES

NOTES

NOTES

NOTES

NOTES